GLOVE AND TRUTH

THE CHRISTIAN MESSAGE

Graham Leighton

Published by Zaccmedia
www.zaccmedia.com
info@zaccmedia.com

Published April 2014

Copyright © 2014 Graham Leighton

The right of Graham Leighton to be identified as author of this work has been asserted by him in accordance with the Copyright, Designs and Patents Act 1988.

All rights reserved. No part of this publication may be reproduced, stored in a retrieval system, or transmitted in any form or by any means, electronic, mechanical, photocopying or otherwise, without the prior written permission of the publisher.

Unless otherwise stated, all Scripture quotations are taken from the Holy Bible, NEW INTERNATIONAL VERSION® Anglicized, NIV® Copyright © 1979, 1984, 2011 by Biblica, Inc.® Used by permission. All rights reserved worldwide.

NEW INTERNATIONAL VERSION® and NIV® are registered trademarks of Biblica, Inc. Use of either trademark for the offering of goods or services requires the prior written consent of Biblica US, Inc.

ISBN: 978-1-909824-31-7

British Library Cataloguing-in-Publication Data
A catalogue record for this book is available from the British Library

Contents

Introduction		v
1	Is It For You?	1
2	The Christian Message	5
3	Ten Stumbling Blocks	41
4	Starting A Relationship With God	75
5	Living The Christian Life	81
6	Some Practical Help	109
Appendix 1: God's Promises and Words of Encouragement		129
Appendix 2: God's Instructions for Christian Living		141
Appendix 3: How the Bible is Structured		151

God's Love and Truth is based entirely on the Holy Bible – God's Word. The Bible translation used for quotations is the New International Version (NIV), 2011 edition.

Introduction

Whoever we are, whatever we are, wherever we find ourselves, our lives are constantly changing. Whether or not we want this to be the case, we cannot stay the same. That is why life is so often described as a journey. We are all heading in one direction or another.

For most of us, there are times when we feel that we are not in control of our lives; we feel as if we are at the mercy of circumstances and forces that are much bigger than we are. And yet, underlying such feelings, deep down, we perhaps recognise that we are not simply a product of our circumstances. The person we become also depends on what matters to us, what we believe, and the choices we make. Ultimately, it is the things that *are* within our control that determine 'who' and 'what' we truly are. These same things also determine whether we are moving in a direction towards God or away from him.

God deeply longs for each of us to come near to him. He in turn will come near to us and embrace us with his overwhelming love and goodness. That is his promise. My hope and prayer is that through the pages of this book you will begin to believe that God knows who you are and passionately cares for you. My yearning is for you to sense something of the extraordinary reality that God is reaching out to you and inviting you into his presence. His burning desire is to love you, make you whole, and restore you to himself.

Come near to God
and he will come near to you.
James 4:8

1

Is It For You?

Above all, the Christian message is a message of supreme love. It is about the God who made us being so overwhelmed by his love for us that he is unable to restrain it, even though we have rejected him. It is about the God who throws open his arms to passionately embrace us, even though we have dirtied and soiled ourselves in his eyes. It is about the God who longs to forgive us, even though we have ignored him and refused to believe in him. It is about the God who has come down to meet us, because he knows we can never work our way up to him. It is about the God of such compassion that he sent his only Son, Jesus Christ, to die in our place and give us an opportunity to go free. It is about the God who raised Jesus back to life again and who in the same way offers each of us a new life.

The Christian message is about the unique person of Jesus Christ. Whoever accepts Jesus accepts God's offer of a renewed relationship with God. Whoever rejects Jesus rejects the only way back to God. We are completely free to decide how to respond to what God is saying; he has given us the right to choose. God, however, is not at all indifferent to our choice. He deeply loves us. He longs for us to know his love, to enter into a relationship with him and to be saved from the mess we are in, but it is up to us. God has given us free will as a loving gift; what we decide to do with it will determine our eternal destiny.

> Whoever has ears, let them hear
> Matthew 11:15

It does not matter who you are, what you are or what you have done. You are of infinite value to God. He is as concerned about you as anyone else on the planet. Your need of him is as great as that of any other person who has ever lived, or ever will live. Whatever your nationality, culture or beliefs – whether you are young or old, wealthy or poor, strong or weak, popular or alone, good or bad – the Christian message is the truth about you and God. There is nothing more important.

God's Love and Truth aims to tell you:

- The complete Christian message; the whole plain truth, without dressing it up
- Who God is and what he is like; his nature, character, desires, purposes and plans
- What a Christian really is; the basis, beginning, life and destiny of a true Christian
- How we stand with God; our choices and their consequences, good and bad

God's Love and Truth aims **not** to:

- Seduce you with tantalising promises
- Condemn you with harsh accusations
- Persuade you with clever arguments
- Patronise you by telling you how you should think, feel or respond
- Deny your unique individuality with sweeping generalisations

God's Love and Truth is firmly based on God's Word, the Holy Bible; inspired by God, written by people.

2

The Christian Message

WHAT IS A CHRISTIAN?

God created the human race out of love. His purpose for us is to live in a close and loving relationship with him. Every single one of us is very special to God, and his burning desire is for friendship with us. The desperate problem is that our relationship with God has been broken. Every one of us is guilty at some point of living life our own way, instead of his. By rejecting him in this way, we shut ourselves off from God.

Despite our rejection of him, God's love for us continues undiminished. So much so that he was willing to go the whole way to mending the relationship. We are naturally separated from God by the wrong in our lives. But God was willing to do something very radical to resolve the problem. In the person

> For if, while we were God's enemies, we were reconciled to him through the death of his Son, how much more, having been reconciled, shall we be saved through his life!
>
> Romans 5:10

of Jesus Christ, God himself entered into our mess with us and did on our behalf what we could never do for ourselves. Jesus died and was raised to life again so that we could be forgiven and start living a new life. God offers every single person the opportunity to get back on track with him and experience his blessing. He offers us the only way to escape the eventual consequences of choosing to stay alienated from God. This is God's greatest gift to the human race. We just have to say 'yes'.

> He was delivered over to death for our sins and was raised to life for our justification. Therefore, since we have been justified through faith, we have peace with God through our Lord Jesus Christ
> Romans 4:25 – 5:1

Christians are people who have come to realise that in God's eyes there is a fundamental problem with their lives, and then done something about it. They have decided to accept God's invitation and allow him to mend the relationship and restore loving friendship. They have entered into a renewed relationship with God, a relationship that starts now and stretches into eternity in heaven. Christians are people who have found peace with God and have decided to start living in agreement with him.

To really make sense of the Christian message we need to go right back to the very start. We need to

> A Christian is someone who believes in Jesus Christ. A Christian is anyone who has decided to trust Jesus to save them from everything wrong in their lives, and has decided to follow his way of living.

discover who God is, what he is like and what he has done. We need to know what has gone wrong with the world and what God has done about it. We also need to understand how we naturally stand with God, the choices we have and the outcome of the decisions we are free to make.

WHO IS GOD?

An expression that remains in common use is 'Oh my god!' For the most part, the phrase probably has little real meaning to those who use it. Nevertheless, it raises a question: who is my god? If we want to have a god there are plenty to choose from! Apart from those portrayed by the world's many religions and spiritual movements, we have the option of creating our own gods. Whenever we attribute god-like status to anything or anyone in our lives, we effectively make them our gods. We may do this deliberately, but more often we do not really notice when things have crept onto centre stage in our lives.

> the LORD is the true God; he is the living God, the eternal King.
> Jeremiah 10:10

In Christianity, God is the God of the Holy Bible. In it God describes himself in rather mysterious terms, for example, 'I AM WHO I AM'. By doing this he is telling us that he is beyond our understanding. He is also saying that he does not need to explain himself to anyone. He claims to be the 'One and Only', the only true God and the living God. Christians believe that there is only one God, that there is no other, and that there is none like him. In other words, God is unique and alone as God. God is so far above us and so far beyond our comprehension that he may seem out of reach. And yet, even though God is surrounded by mystery, he is really there and he longs for us to know him.

WHAT IS GOD LIKE?

> Now the Lord is the Spirit, and where the Spirit of the Lord is, there is freedom.
> 2 Corinthians 3:17

The created world we see around us is physical in nature. God's nature is not physical but spiritual, and we cannot see him. Although he is spirit he is not some impersonal force, but rather a personal loving being who longs to be known by the people he has made. He is therefore a God who reveals himself to us and he wants us to know him personally.

God of love and relationships

Relationships are extremely important to God. This can be seen from a mysterious aspect of God's nature: his three-part make-up. He is just one God but also three different Persons, all at the same time; God the Father, Jesus Christ his Son, and the Holy Spirit. Within himself, amongst these three Persons, there is a relationship of selfless love. It is this desire to relate and to love that led him to create us, so that he could love us and relate to us.

> let us love one another, for love comes from God. Everyone who loves has been born of God and knows God. Whoever does not love does not know God, for God is love.
> 1 John 4:7–8

Love lies at the very centre of God's nature. God is much more than just loving; the Bible tells us that he *is* love. In other words, love is a central part of God's make-up. Love is one of God's greatest gifts to the world. In fact, all true love that anyone ever experiences actually emanates from God. Love has a source and that source is God. People often wonder where evil comes from, but they seldom seem to wonder about the source of love. Where does love come from? Love comes from God!

> Give thanks to the LORD, for he is good; his love endures for ever.
> Psalm 107:1

God's love for us is one of overwhelming passion. He has a burning desire to be with us and enjoy a close and intimate relationship with us. God is a God of deep feelings and strong emotions. The good feelings and positive emotions we experience reflect the nature of God in us, as he made us. Our desire to love and be loved comes from him. He is not a distant and cold God but one of deep affection, warmth, understanding and tenderness. God's love governs his whole attitude towards us; he is patient and kind, generous and merciful, compassionate and gentle.

> God demonstrates his own love for us in this: while we were still sinners, Christ died for us.
> Romans 5:8

The reality of God's love for us was supremely demonstrated in the person of Jesus Christ. It was out of love that God the Father gave Jesus to us so that our broken relationship with him could be mended. It was out of love that Jesus reached out to people with compassion and healed them from all kinds of illnesses and oppressions. Above all, God showed us the infinite depth of his love for us by the selfless giving of one life for another. In Jesus Christ God gave us everything; he gave up his life in place of ours so that we might live.

Glorious Creator

Creativeness lies deep within the heart of God. He defines what it means to have an imagination; he envisions things that do not exist, he

> You are worthy, our Lord and God, to receive glory and honour and power, for you created all things, and by your will they were created and have their being.
> Revelation 4:11

designs them, and then he makes them out of nothing. He put light into the darkness, created the earth where there was only a void, formed skies around the earth, placed seas on its surface, and populated the air, land and water with every conceivable type of plant and animal. Finally, having made everything else ready, he made the pinnacle of his creation, something very special, formed in his own likeness: he made us. He gave his wonderful creation to us to enjoy and he entrusted us to look after it.

> Who among the gods is like you, LORD? Who is like you – majestic in holiness, awesome in glory, working wonders?
> Exodus 15:11

The wonder of God's creation envelops us. Above us, the overwhelming vastness of intergalactic space where stars are born and combine into mesmerizingly beautiful galaxies extending through all space and time. Around us, the breathtaking majesty of mountain peaks, enchanting landscapes, and a fascinating and endless assortment of living creatures. And inside us, the miracle of life, the incomprehensible complexity of countless billions of atoms working together to form a living, breathing, walking, talking, thinking, feeling person.

Whenever we look around us and notice the splendour and beauty of the natural world, we get just a glimpse of the true glory of its Maker. God is of unparalleled beauty and majesty. Those in the Bible who had visions of God struggled helplessly to find words to describe the dazzling glory of his appearance. When we stop and take time to notice, it is possible to experience special moments when the natural beauty in creation bursts through to leave us in awe. When we are moved by the beauty of the world, we are sensing something of the pleasure God himself derives from his amazing creation.

Caring Provider

God actively cares for his creation. His love for us is much more than just feelings and emotions; it is highly practical and it leads

> He causes his sun to rise on the evil and the good, and sends rain on the righteous and the unrighteous.
> Matthew 5:45

him directly into action. He is the ultimate Provider of all we need to live. Each day he creates new life and continues to give life to every living thing on earth. God is the source of all life; without him everything would die. No-one else can create things out of nothing and breathe life into them, no-one else can sustain life in all that lives; God alone can do all this. Without God's creative power there would be no resources for us to make anything out of. Without him giving life to plants and animals there would be nothing to eat. Without him giving power to our bodies to heal themselves, there would be no recovery from injury or illness. God lovingly provides all this and so much more for the benefit of all: those who love him and equally those who do not.

> The God who made the world and everything in it is the Lord of heaven and earth and does not live in temples built by human hands. And he is not served by human hands, as if he needed anything. Rather, he himself gives everyone life and breath and everything else.
> Acts 17:24-25

Powerful Ruler

God has entrusted the world to us, and we have made a mess of it. Despite appearances, God is in control. He is the absolute Ruler who rules over his creation with love. He safely nurtures his creation in his powerful and loving hands. Every authority on earth is ultimately subject to him. He rules over the present and he governs the future, directing everything towards the fulfilment of his eternal plan. He empowers people to do good, sets limits for evil and turns evil into good. God exercises his powerful rule with love and restraint for the good of all.

God is great; he has unlimited power. He is so powerful that simply by speaking some commands, creation came into being. The stars and planets appear and disappear; they move through space and God holds each one in its place. He is also unlimited in his presence. He is not confined by space or time as we are. His home is in heaven, but his presence extends to fill all of creation throughout all of time; he is everywhere. King David, who wrote the Psalms, said, 'Where can I flee from your presence?' The answer is nowhere. When God described himself as the Alpha and the Omega he meant that he is without beginning or end. God lives outside of time; he is eternal. He is the everlasting and unchanging God, the same yesterday and today and forever.

> Now to the King eternal, immortal, invisible, the only God, be honour and glory for ever and ever. Amen.
> 1 Timothy 1:17

Our Creator knows and understands us in a way no-one else ever could. His infinite nature enables him to know absolutely everything about everyone all of the time. He knows our every thought, word, action, desire, attitude, motive and intention. The Spirit of God searches people's

> Nothing in all creation is hidden from God's sight. Everything is uncovered and laid bare before the eyes of him to whom we must give account.
> Hebrews 4:13

hearts; nothing is hidden from him and he cannot be deceived. Before him we are completely laid bare and exposed for what we really are, and yet he still deeply loves us. God is the Almighty God. One day all of creation will come face to face with him and will bow down before him in awe.

Perfect in holiness

> He is the Rock, his works are perfect, and all his ways are just. A faithful God who does no wrong, upright and just is he.
> Deuteronomy 32:4

A God with unlimited knowledge and power has the potential to be very fearsome and terrifying, so can God be trusted with such awesome ability? The answer is yes, he can be completely trusted, because he is perfect. There is absolutely no fault to be found in God, not even the slightest trace of anything wrong. He always does whatever is completely right and his motives are always uncompromisingly good and pure. Together, these qualities begin to describe God's holiness. In fact God is so utterly holy that he is actually incapable of doing wrong.

His holiness also means that it is impossible for him to intimately embrace any-

> God is light; in him there is no darkness at all.
> 1 John 1:5

thing that is any less holy than he is. If he did, he would be tainted. God's holy nature dictates that he must remain utterly separate from all that is wrong. God uses words such as 'unclean', 'impure' and 'defiled' to describe anything or anyone that is less holy than he is. These words picture the spoiling effect that wrongdoing, or 'sin', has on the world and everything in it. Anyone who is less perfect than God is unholy, and since God alone is perfect that means everyone.

The contrast between holy and unholy is portrayed as a comparison between light and dark. God is light, and outside of him is a spiritual darkness.

Upholder of justice

Kindness and benevolence flow out of God's love, but his love is not sentimental. It coexists in complete

> For he will deliver the needy who cry out, the afflicted who have no one to help. He will take pity on the weak
> Psalm 72:12–13

harmony with his holiness and justice. God's justice will one day cause him to pass judgement on all that is wrong. The wrongs will be put right and all the injustices of the world will finally be overturned. Until then, this same sense of faultless justice leads him to defend the oppressed and go to the aid of the needy. God's eyes are on those who are bowed down and he offers them his help and strength.

> Blessed is the one whom God corrects; so do not despise the discipline of the Almighty.
> Job 5:17

Guiding Parent

God's love for us prevents him from abandoning us to the effects of all our short-

comings. He loves us as we are and he opens his arms to accept us if we will turn to him, but he does not want us to stay this way. He wants to save us from ourselves and change us. True love must intervene and not just stand back. So God guides us and disciplines us in order to bring us closer to himself. He wants those who reject him to realise just how desperately they need him and to change their minds about him. He wants those who do know him to become more like him and to be prepared for life in heaven. God's love is utterly faithful; he perseveres with us and never gives up.

So, what is God like?

> The LORD, the LORD, the compassionate and gracious God, slow to anger, abounding in love and faithfulness, maintaining love to thousands, and forgiving wickedness, rebellion and sin.
> *Exodus 34:6–7*

He is the only true and living God, God of love, Creator of all things, awesome in his power and glory, completely perfect, without fault or failing, utterly opposed to all that is wrong, the righteous Judge to whom all must answer, yet the compassionate and gracious one, the God who saves, who shows mercy, who forgives, and who offers a fresh start and eternal happiness to all who will listen to him and turn to him.

GOD AND US – HOW DO WE STAND?

> you were dead in your transgressions and sins, in which you used to live when you followed the ways of this world ... gratifying the cravings of our flesh and following its desires and thoughts. Like the rest, we were by nature deserving of wrath.
> *Ephesians 2:1–3*

In the Bible, God plainly tells us how we naturally stand with him, and it is a sad picture. God created the human race to enjoy a very special loving relationship with him, but the relationship has been broken. The human race has rejected God and decided to live its own way. God created people out of love, but they have rebelled against him and rejected him. As a result our natural state is one of spiritual deadness and alienation from God.

> Whoever sows to please their flesh, from the flesh will reap destruction ...
> *Galatians 6:8*

God also warns us how things will turn out if we choose to remain in this position. We will be subject to his judgement and will face the awful prospect of being completely separated from his goodness forever. If we insist on clinging on to all that is wrong in us, then, much as it pains him, God will be forced to finally release us into the grip of what we have chosen.

> ... whoever sows to please the Spirit, from the Spirit will reap eternal life.
> Galatians 6:8

The alternative is to change our minds about God and return to him. This is what God calls every single person to do. Those who respond to God are immediately reconciled to him and forgiven. They receive new spiritual life and their relationship with God is restored. Their position before God is permanently changed. When the time comes, these people will escape God's judgement. Instead they will be rewarded for their faith and enjoy a future of joy and happiness in God's presence forever. In other words their destiny is eternal life in heaven.

If this really is the situation, why is it? How did we get into this mess?

When God created us he made us in his own image. This means he blessed us with

> We love because he first loved us.
> 1 John 4:19

certain special characteristics that we have in common with his own nature and that differentiate us from all the other living creatures he made. These include the capacity to make moral judgements and a spirit that will never die. God's nature is to love and he made us for this very reason: for him to love us first and for us to love him in return. His desire is for a joyful and fulfilling relationship between himself as our Creator and us, his much loved creation.

THE CHRISTIAN MESSAGE

> Whoever believes and is baptised will be saved, but whoever does not believe will be condemned.
> *Mark 16:16*

To make such a relationship possible, God needed to give us something else, a characteristic of extreme importance. He gave us free will; he gave us the right to choose. God did not want to create machines programmed to obey. This would not have been a relationship of love, but rather one of master and slave. God gave us free will so we could voluntarily choose to accept him and love him back.

> God saw all that he had made, and it was very good.
> *Genesis 1:31*

This is where our problem begins. The world has chosen to reject God. The very first people God made, at the beginning of time, were born into a perfect relationship with him. There were no barriers between them and God; they were completely free from every impurity.

> Once you were alienated from God and were enemies in your minds because of your evil behaviour.
> *Colossians 1:21*

Sadly, these people decided to exercise God's gift of free will to step outside the protective boundaries he had given them. They disobeyed God and in so doing rebelled against him. They decided they knew better than God and did things their own way instead of his. In other words they 'sinned' against God. In the process their human natures became corrupted by their disobedience and so they brought God's holy judgement upon themselves. These people were God's most precious creation; with great sadness he was forced to banish them from the intimacy of his full presence.

> sin entered the world through one man, and death through sin, and in this way death came to all people, because all sinned
> Romans 5:12

The actions of the first people impact on all of us. We are all ultimately descended from the first created people of God. So we inherit something of what has gone before; we inherit their spiritual condition. When the first people disobeyed God they corrupted themselves, sin entered them, and through them sin entered the whole human race. This spiritual corruption of our nature is our inherited condition. We are all born imperfect, contaminated by sin. We are born belonging to a race of people who in their natural state are separated from God. We are born needing to be saved.

Although we inherit an imperfect nature we also inherit God's gift of free will. Therefore, we remain completely responsible to God for our individual actions. We can choose to follow our wrong inclinations or to follow God. We can choose to stay separated from him or to be reconciled to him. We are free to make our own personal choices and we are accountable to God for our own lives.

What is sin?

> Everyone who sins breaks the law; in fact, sin is lawlessness ...
> All wrongdoing is sin
> 1 John 3:4; 5:17

God created us and knows what is best for us. God's intention is for us to enjoy true happiness and fulfilment under his full blessing. Therefore, he has set boundaries for us, not to frustrate us or to rob us of anything good, but in order to protect us from the things that harm us. Sin is any departure from God's perfect way of living. It is anything that we do, say or simply think that ruins God's perfect design.

THE CHRISTIAN MESSAGE

When we behave this way we are living under self-rule rather than God's rule, and the underlying attitudes are those of pride and selfishness. Every wrong act spoils and corrupts God's perfect creation. It robs us of joy and, if not dealt with, it would eventually destroy us. Whatever form it takes, any departure from God's plan ultimately leads into unhappiness, not happiness, and into frustration, not fulfilment.

> 'Love the Lord your God with all your heart and with all your soul and with all your mind.' This is the first and greatest commandment. And the second is like it: 'Love your neighbour as yourself.'
> Matthew 22:37–39

The bounds of sin extend even further than this. Its limits do not end with the things we do wrong; it also includes the things we do not do. God not only wants to bless us, but he also wants us to be a blessing. He wants us to bless him back and to bless everyone else around us as well. Therefore, we also miss the mark when we fall short in our love for God, or in our love for others. The word 'sin' may seem odd and outdated to many people, but there is really no other word that is encompassing enough to properly encapsulate the full extent of the human condition it refers to.

The evidence of the presence of sin in the world is overwhelming; it is directly or indirectly responsible for all of the world's problems. There are the deliberate wrong things people do, such as: violence, theft, child abuse, rape, drug and alcohol abuse, fraud, sexual abuse,

> The LORD saw how great the wickedness of the human race had become on the earth, and that every inclination of the thoughts of the human heart was only evil all the time. The LORD regretted that he had made human beings on the earth, and his heart was deeply troubled.
> Genesis 6:5–6

wars and conflicts, terrorist attacks, blackmail, vandalism, muggings, child pornography, racism, abuse of power – the list goes on and on. Then there are all the unintentional things people do wrong through ignorance, human error and human weakness. The effect of sin has even affected the workings of our planet and our own bodies. So to our list we can add earthquakes, floods, hurricanes, famines, droughts, catastrophic accidents, illnesses, diseases, injuries, and so much more.

There are so many problems in the world, causing so much misery to so many people. Each day the news proclaims the sad story of the effects of all this wrong. None of these problems existed in the perfect world God originally made. It is impossible to escape the glaringly obvious conclusion that there is something dreadfully wrong with the world we now live in. The problem is the presence of sin.

> For it is from within, out of a person's heart, that evil thoughts come – sexual immorality, theft, murder, adultery, greed, malice, deceit, lewdness, envy, slander, arrogance and folly. All these evils come from inside and defile a person.
> Mark 7:21–23

If the evidence of sin is obvious on a worldwide scale, then it is equally obvious at a personal level. It is all too often apparent in our words and actions, both in the things we say and do, and in the things we do *not* say and do. When we observe each other we can often detect at least traces of pride or arrogance, self-centredness, greed, foul language, laziness, lust, selfish ambition, anger, jealousy, deceit, spite, meanness, malicious gossip, impatience, intolerance, lack of compassion and care – to name just a few unpleasant sides to human behaviour.

> the LORD searches every heart and understands every desire and every thought.
> 1 Chronicles 28:9

If we dare to examine *ourselves* in the light of God's holy standards, we will discover just how sullied we really are. Those around us may notice some of the things that are wrong with us. Fortunately for us, they see just a fraction of the real truth; indeed we cannot even see it ourselves, but God sees it all. The outward evidence is only the outflow of the root of sin that is buried inside us; some of it seeps out, but a lot remains hidden. The real problem lies deep within; it lies within those black attitudes in our hearts and our inherited tendency to resist God.

> If we claim to be without sin, we deceive ourselves and the truth is not in us.
> 1 John 1:8

Whether we realise it or not, we are all guilty of going against God. When we do things our own way instead of his, we are saying we know better than him. When we accept all the benefits of his goodness whilst denying him as the Provider, we are abusing his grace. When we dedicate ourselves to the pursuit of fulfilment through worldly things, we are worshipping created things rather than the Creator. If we do not accept God, we are saying we do not believe that he loves us and that he intends the very best for us; we are calling him a liar.

> There is no one righteous, not even one; there is no one who understands ... no one who seeks God. All have turned away
> Romans 3:10–12

At some point we have all chosen to try and live lives of independence instead of dependence on God. When we do this we are at heart self-centred instead of God-centred. We in effect depose him from his rightful place as Lord of our lives and usurp the place for ourselves. Before God we appear proud and selfish. Through these actions and attitudes we are actually rejecting God and rebelling against him.

> Today, if you hear his voice, do not harden your hearts.
> Hebrews 4:7

A witness to the truth of this is the prick of our conscience inside us, our God-given instinct that convicts us when things are not as they should be. The witness of our conscience can be powerful, yet it can easily lose its impact on us. The further away from God we drift, then the easier it becomes to ignore him. The longer we stay away from him, the easier it is to convince ourselves everything is alright, when it isn't. When this happens we live a lie, persuading ourselves to believe we are right, when we are wrong. We can become so numbed and insensitive that God's truth seldom penetrates. This is why it is so important to respond to God's truth whenever it reaches us.

Why does sin matter?

God is completely just and his justice means that every wrong carries a penalty. He cannot simply ignore sin as

> There is only one Lawgiver and Judge, the one who is able to save and destroy.
> James 4:12

if it did not exist or did not matter; it must be dealt with. Somehow our guilt needs to be removed from us. One day everyone will be confronted with the reality of their sin, the way God sees it, and will be compelled to agree that his judgement is fair – because God is right.

We need to be made holy like God. In his love and

mercy God has provided a way for this to happen. He sent Jesus Christ to pay the penalty for us. Through Jesus, God offers us the chance to be saved from judgement. Everyone who decides to accept God's offer can face him with utter confidence, because every wrong in their lives will have been washed away. In God's sight they will be completely clean because Jesus will have purified them.

> at that time you were separate from Christ, excluded from citizenship ... without hope and without God in the world.
> Ephesians 2:12

We have a choice – what is it?

The loving friendship God intended us to have with him has been broken; we are separated from God. The choice we have is whether to stay this way, or to be reconciled to God and enter into a new relationship with him. After our natural bodies die there is an eternal existence. Depending on the decision we make, this existence will either be one of blessing in God's presence, or one where we suffer the effects of separation from him. This is what *hell* actually is; an existence completely shut off from the love and goodness of God's life-giving presence.

What separates us from God is our spiritually corrupted condition. God is perfect and he cannot be united with anything that has been spoiled. Any blemish, no matter how small, is a blemish too much. Just one tiny failing in our lives and we are spiritually ruined. The only way we can be reunited with God is for it to be as if we were made perfect again. To do this for ourselves we would need to completely remove every effect of everything that is wrong about us: the imperfect nature we were born with and the consequences of every mistake we had ever made. Every slightest trace of anything wrong we have ever said, thought or done would need to be obliterated. Then, having done all this, we would need to start living utterly perfect lives!

> For whoever keeps the whole law and yet stumbles at just one point is guilty of breaking all of it.
> James 2:10

The crushing problem for us is that we are completely unable to do this. Suppose by some mega effort we were to suddenly start living utterly pure and holy lives – it would only be a very short space of time before we lapsed. The slightest hint of pride or selfishness or resentment or jealousy or desire to retaliate or self-pity. The merest trace of sexual immorality or impurity, any neglect in glorifying God or serving him completely or loving others as ourselves, and we would fail. It is an impossible task.

> for all have sinned and fall short of the glory of God
> Romans 3:23

Even if it were possible to start living a perfect life it would still not be enough. Why? Because we would have done nothing to put right all the wrongs of our past. Nor would we have changed the spoiled nature we were born with. We are stained and we cannot make ourselves clean. No matter how good our intentions, no matter how much effort we make to change, no matter how hard we try to please others, nothing will enable us to make God's grade – utter perfection. This then is the *bad news*; in our own hands our situation is completely hopeless.

Fortunately there is also *good news* – this is the Christian

> God made him who had no sin to be sin for us, so that in him we might become the righteousness of God
> 2 Corinthians 5:21

message! The good news is that what we are unable do for ourselves God has done for us. God is loving; he is merciful and kind, he is patient and understanding. He longs to forgive us because he loves us so much and because he passionately desires the very best for us. Although he is deeply hurt by our disobedience he wants to bring every single person back to himself. However, his holiness and justice demand that sin be paid for. It cannot be ignored or overlooked, it must be dealt with; justice must be done. Therefore God's answer to our predicament was to satisfy the requirement for justice himself. There was a penalty to pay and he has paid it for us.

> For the wages of sin is death, but the gift of God is eternal life in Christ Jesus our Lord.
> Romans 6:23

The Bible tells us that the wages of sin is death – an everlasting existence completely separated from the life, love and goodness of God. This is the penalty that we all face. Suppose, however, that someone could take our place and die on our behalf as our substitute, a sacrifice to God that would satisfy God's justice. Suppose further that this substitute was utterly perfect, completely without blemish. What would an act such as this achieve? The answer is that such an act would take away the sins of the world. Every lapse, by every person, for all time, past, present and future would be paid for. Why? Because the sacrifice was perfect!

This is exactly what God has done. He sent Jesus Christ, the Son of God the

> For God so loved the world that he gave his one and only Son, that whoever believes in him shall not perish but have eternal life. For God did not send his Son into the world to condemn the world, but to save the world through him.
> John 3:16-17

Father, God himself, to come as a man. An utterly unique person, fully God and fully man, perfect and without fault, to die in our place. Jesus has opened up a way for us to get back to God. Through him we are all offered the opportunity to be saved from our sin.

THE CHRISTIAN 'GOOD NEWS' IS A PERSON – JESUS CHRIST

To many people, Jesus Christ is nothing more than a historical figure who lived 2,000 years ago. Quite possibly the most famous person of all time, someone who even today has a large following. A good man and a great moral teacher, a man who was killed by crucifixion, probably unjustly, a martyr for his cause. All in all, an extraordinary man, but for all that, just a man.

> For in Christ all the fullness of the Deity lives in bodily form
> *Colossians 2:9*

It is true that Jesus holds a very special place in history, but there is much more to this person than that. Jesus is completely unique. He was not only a man but also God, and he not only lived then, he lives today. He is the Son of God whom the Father sent into the world. God became a man to live amongst us. He did this for a very specific purpose: to save us. The name 'Jesus' means 'God saves', and 'Christ' means 'anointed by God'. He was also called 'Immanuel', which means 'God with us'. Jesus Christ is God our Saviour come to earth as a man.

> I bring you good news that will cause great joy for all the people. Today in the town of David a Saviour is born to you; he is the Messiah, the Lord.
> *Luke 2:10–11*

Jesus did not suddenly arrive on earth as a fully

grown person ready to launch into his task of saving the world. God's purpose for Jesus required that he enter into complete identification with humanity; he had to become completely man and completely God at the same time. So the starting point for the Christ on earth was the same as for all of us: he had to be born. The unique nature of this union between God and humanity was reflected in his miraculous conception; conceived by the Holy Spirit in a human mother, Mary.

The birth of Jesus was of momentous importance to God and to the world. We might have expected God to have grabbed the world's attention, brought us into a place of awe, and surrounded the birth with great splendour and adulation. But this was not to be the manner of God's coming. In Jesus Christ, God stooped down to meet us; he made himself low, he humbled himself and entered quietly into our mess and our ordinariness. Christ was born in obscurity, in a small town crammed full of visitors, where there was no place for his pregnant mother to stay. Unnoticed by the bustling and hectic world, Jesus was born in a place where animals were kept. But heaven did notice. At his birth all heaven rejoiced; the long-awaited plan of God had swung into action, God's favour now rested on the world and a special peace fell over the place where he lay.

> Suddenly a great company of the heavenly host appeared with the angel, praising God and saying, 'Glory to God in the highest heaven, and on earth peace to those on whom his favour rests.'
> Luke 2:13–14

Following this supernatural beginning, the life of Jesus was outwardly very ordinary. He

> Jesus grew in wisdom and stature, and in favour with God and man.
> Luke 2:52

lived in a small town with his mother Mary and her husband Joseph, together with his brothers and sisters, learning a craft as a carpenter. But at the same time a very special boy who did no wrong. One in whom was the very character of God himself, one who lived in a unique relationship with his heavenly Father. Gradually, Jesus grew up. He grew in understanding of who he really was, the Christ. He grew in character, in wisdom, in knowledge and in strength. Jesus grew up, quietly and peacefully, in submission and obedience to God the Father. Never did he err, never was his divine goodness marred in any way; he was the perfect Son of God.

Things were to change dramatically for Jesus in his early thirties. The time to emerge from obscurity had arrived. It was time for God to reveal to the world who Jesus really was and why he had come. The Holy Spirit descended on Jesus in power. He was entrusted with the full authority of God his Father. But could Jesus really be trusted with such awesome power?

> And as he was praying, heaven was opened and the Holy Spirit descended on him in bodily form like a dove. And a voice came from heaven: 'You are my Son, whom I love; with you I am well pleased.'
> Luke 3:21–22

To answer this, God allowed Jesus to endure a time of severe testing. Jesus was led by the Holy Spirit into a desert. There he encountered evil personified in the form of the devil, the enemy of God who is called Satan. For forty days and nights, with nothing

> For we do not have a high priest who is unable to feel sympathy for our weaknesses, but we have one who has been tempted in every way, just as we are – yet he did not sin.
> Hebrews 4:15

to eat, the full force of this evil enemy was unleashed against him. The Son of God, confined to a human body, was taken to the limits of human exhaustion. He was goaded and subjected to intense temptations to misuse his true position and power. But at the end of all this, Jesus remained completely faultless. Satan had never met such a man, one who could utterly resist him. Jesus showed that he was completely pure and unselfish. He showed that he wholeheartedly sought to serve and glorify God and not himself. Jesus demonstrated that he had total faith in God his Father and that he would trust and obey him completely, without reserve.

> the Son of Man did not come to be served, but to serve, and to give his life as a ransom for many.
> Matthew 20:28

In Jesus Christ the world saw at first hand what God is like. The world also saw what mankind is meant to be like. Jesus revealed the nature of a human being as God originally created us to be. Jesus overflowed with love and deep compassion. He was humble and gentle of heart, a person completely at peace with who he was. A person with intense feelings yet calm and in control. A person of infinite goodness, devoting himself to God and others, sacrificing himself over and over again. In heaven Jesus had enjoyed his position of Lordship. He was the majestic and glorious King and worthy of all honour and praise. Now the King had become a servant, completely submitted to his Father's will, pouring himself out for us.

Jesus mixed with all kinds of people and reached out to them with understanding.

> Jesus returned to Galilee in the power of the Spirit, and news about him spread through the whole countryside.
> Luke 4:14

GOD'S LOVE AND TRUTH

He saw their needs and was moved. He touched their hearts and he healed their minds and bodies. The blind were able to see again, the deaf could hear, the paralysed walked and those trapped in inner torment were set free and given peace.

Through his miracles Jesus demonstrated the love and power of God, and the people were amazed.

Those who stopped to listen were captivated by the wisdom and colourfulness of Jesus' teaching. He brought a message, not of condemnation, but of mercy and forgiveness, a message of love. He spoke hope and freedom into people's lives. Wherever he went Jesus revealed the truth about God and the truth about men and women. He proclaimed the true meaning of his coming, the good news of the opportunity to return to God and be reconciled to him.

So what reception did this unique person receive? By many he was enthusiastically received. To them his words were like streams of living water, bringing deep refreshment to parched lives. He brought hope, he brought healing, he brought freedom and deliverance. Crowds followed him, gasping to hear the truth and wisdom of his teaching. They were touched deeply by his love and

> Jesus went through all the towns and villages, teaching in their synagogues, proclaiming the good news of the kingdom and healing every disease and illness. When he saw the crowds, he had compassion on them, because they were harassed and helpless, like sheep without a shepherd.
> Matthew 9:35–36

> Everyone who drinks this water will be thirsty again, but whoever drinks the water I give them will never thirst. Indeed, the water I give them will become in them a spring of water welling up to eternal life.
> John 4:13–14

THE CHRISTIAN MESSAGE

compassion, and amazed by his miracles. These were the people who would listen, who were open and receptive, who were prepared to face up to the truth about themselves and about God. These were the people with the faith to believe. To them Jesus brought healing and forgiveness, freedom from the past, joy in the present and a future of eternal happiness.

But only a few accepted Jesus; by the majority he was rejected. The religious leaders, his own nation and people of all races rejected and despised him. They ridiculed and mocked him, they judged and condemned him, they called him a liar and they lied about him. The light of the world was amongst them. In his light men and women felt exposed and they resented it. These were the people who would not listen, who closed their minds and hardened their hearts. People of pride and selfishness, who were stubborn and unyielding. People who deluded themselves, who would not face up to the truth about themselves and about God. People of unbelief who refused God.

> This is the verdict: light has come into the world, but people loved darkness instead of light because their deeds were evil. Everyone who does evil hates the light, and will not come into the light for fear that their deeds will be exposed.
> John 3:19–20

The worst of these people set out to persecute Jesus, to bring him down and crush him. So it was that they opened themselves instead to evil; by refusing God they sided with his enemy. Satan found unwitting allies amongst men and women, and he inspired

> When they came to the place called the Skull, they crucified him there ... Jesus said, 'Father, forgive them, for they do not know what they are doing.'
> Luke 23:33–34

them and goaded them onward. They plotted and planned, they lied and deceived, they worked to destroy Jesus, and finally they brought him to a wooden cross where they crucified him.

Jesus Christ, whom God had sent into the world to save it, was whipped and beaten, mocked and spat on, tried as a criminal and sentenced to death. The raging crowd, incensed with evil, dragged Jesus away and they killed him. Yet throughout all this the Son of God humbled himself before God and the world. He had the infinite power of God at his disposal; he had legions of mighty angels at his command. Yet he made no objections, he made no defence, he did not resist, he did not retaliate. Instead he entrusted himself completely to God his Father, the Mighty Ruler over all creation. Satan had done his worst. Jesus was dead.

> who, being in very nature God, did not consider equality with God something to be used to his own advantage; rather, he made himself nothing by taking the very nature of a servant, being made in human likeness. And being found in appearance as a man, he humbled himself by becoming obedient to death – even death on a cross!
> *Philippians 2:6–8*

Evil appeared to reign, but from the very beginning it was God's plan that Jesus should die. What Satan intended for Jesus' defeat, God had planned for his victory. The sin of the world had to be dealt with. God's justice had to be satisfied. What could possibly pay the price for our disobedience and remove the penalty that was on all of us? Only a perfect substitute, only the perfect Son of God, only Jesus Christ could take our place.

> This is love: not that we loved God, but that he loved us and sent his Son as an atoning sacrifice for our sins.
> *1 John 4:10*

THE CHRISTIAN MESSAGE

> Is it nothing to you, all you who pass by? Look around and see. Is any suffering like my suffering that was inflicted on me, that the LORD brought on me in the day of his fierce anger?
>
> Lamentations 1:12

As Jesus hung dying on the cross, his suffering was beyond our comprehension. The extent of his suffering was not merely the excruciating physical pain he endured. Nor was it just the deep emotional distress of being rejected by the people he loved so much. The worst of it was the unimaginable weight of the sins of the whole world for all time that bore down on him.

Our failings crushed the holy Son of God. He became sin for us and the sin that was on him was so great

> For Christ also suffered once for sins, the righteous for the unrighteous, to bring you to God.
>
> 1 Peter 3:18

that God his Father withdrew his presence from him. In the midst of such inner desolation, Jesus Christ died for all of us. In death the blood that Jesus shed satisfied the Father's justice and opened up the way back to God for those who would believe.

> God raised him from the dead, freeing him from the agony of death, because it was impossible for death to keep its hold on him.
>
> Acts 2:24

It was God's plan that Jesus should die, but it was not God's plan that Jesus should stay dead. On the third day after his crucifixion God raised Jesus Christ back to life. Jesus' dead body was placed in a new tomb, but he emerged from the tomb a mighty victor; the tomb is empty. Jesus Christ is victorious over sin, victorious over death and victorious over hell, and by the grace of God we are invited to share in his victory!

GOD'S LOVE AND TRUTH

> Therefore God exalted him to the highest place and gave him the name that is above every name, that at the name of Jesus every knee should bow, in heaven and on earth and under the earth, and every tongue acknowledge that Jesus Christ is Lord, to the glory of God the Father.
> *Philippians 2:9–11*

Hundreds of people saw the risen Jesus. Over a period of forty days his disciples and many others met him, talked to him and ate with him. Finally, before their eyes, in the presence of angels, Jesus returned home. Jesus has been restored to his rightful place of glory and honour in heaven where he sits at the right hand of God the Father. Jesus Christ is Lord and he is worthy of all our worship and praise.

Jesus promised never to leave us. Shortly after his ascension back into heaven, he sent the promised Holy Spirit into the world.

> And I will ask the Father, and he will give you another advocate to help you and be with you for ever – the Spirit of truth
> *John 14:16–17*

Those who believed in Jesus had lost his physical presence, but they were to gain something even better. On the day of Pentecost the Holy Spirit came down from heaven and filled every believer in Jesus. The Spirit of Jesus had come into the world to be with every Christian forever. On that day the Christian church was born.

> And if I go and prepare a place for you, I will come back and take you to be with me that you also may be where I am.
> *John 14:3*

Jesus has promised to return. When he does, he will judge the present world and establish his kingdom in full. Everything will be renewed and made perfect as it was in the beginning. The first time Jesus came, it was in humility as a servant. The next time he comes, it will be in glory and majesty as Lord and King. At that time all of creation will recognise Jesus Christ for who he really is: Lord of lords and King of kings.

> This is what is written: the Messiah will suffer and rise from the dead on the third day, and repentance for the forgiveness of sins will be preached in his name to all nations
> Luke 24:46–47

Jesus Christ entered the world to save us all by dying on our behalf. He took our place and has paid the penalty of our guilt for us. He has opened up a way for us to get back to God; through Jesus, God offers to save every single person. Whoever believes in Jesus Christ and accepts him in faith will be saved. They will belong to Christ; they will receive the Holy Spirit and have eternal life.

WHAT MAKES A PERSON A CHRISTIAN – AND WHAT DOESN'T?

God created every one of us to enjoy a very special loving relationship with him, but the relationship has been broken. The *bad news* is that in our natural state we are all separated from God by all our failings and shortcomings, and we are destined to face his judgement. What is more, we are completely helpless to do anything about it for ourselves.

> Jesus said to her, 'I am the resurrection and the life. The one who believes in me will live'
> John 11:25

The *good news* is that what we cannot do for ourselves God has done for us. Through Jesus Christ, God has made it possible for us to be saved from his judgement and reconciled to himself. This is the Christian message, the gospel of God.

What takes us from one position before God into the

other? From unsaved to saved? From being destined to an existence without God to a destiny of life with God in heaven? There are many misconceptions about what makes a person a Christian. Here are some of the things that do *not* make a person a Christian:

- Believing in God's existence
- Going to church
- Reading the Bible
- Doing your best to live a good and honest life
- Trying to live by the Ten Commandments
- Helping others and showing kindness
- Giving generously to charity
- Praying
- Singing hymns or worship songs
- Being born in a 'Christian' country
- Being christened
- Being baptised
- Being brought up in a Christian home
- Having a religious education
- Getting married in church
- Taking part in Communion
- Reading religious books
- Watching religious programmes

> But when the kindness and love of God our Saviour appeared, he saved us, not because of righteous things we had done, but because of his mercy.
> Titus 3:4–5

None of the above has ever made a person a Christian and none of the above ever will. It is true that many of these things are admirable. It is also true that many of these things are consistent with Christian teaching and are exactly what committed Christians believe in doing. Nevertheless, no matter how right these things may be for people to do, either before they have become Christians or afterwards, they do not *make* a person a Christian. So what does?

Before answering this question it is worth summarising the Christian message:

- God is the One and Only God. He is all-powerful, completely perfect, and above all he is love. God created us to live in a perfect loving relationship with him and experience his full blessing. He gave us moral understanding, free will, and a spirit that lives forever.
- God provided boundaries to protect us and enable us to live in happiness. But from the very beginning, the people God created doubted him and decided to go their own way instead of his. God's perfection was spoiled. Pain and death entered the world. God views this rejection of himself as rebellion and he calls it sin. Every single person is born with the effects of sin. We all live imperfect lives and have this guilt hanging over us.
- God's justice demands that all wrongs are paid for. He is the God of love and mercy, but he is also holy and just. He cannot simply ignore our offences; they must be dealt with. God's judgement finds that we are all guilty. Therefore, we all face the penalty for our failings: eternal separation from God's love and goodness. We are completely powerless to save ourselves from this predicament.
- God's love for us is unlimited. Out of his love, he chose to pay the penalty for us. He made it possible for us to

be saved from his own judgement and enjoy eternal happiness instead. Jesus Christ left heaven, entered the world as a man, lived an unblemished life and died on a cross on our behalf. He took our place and paid the price of our guilt for us.

- Jesus was raised to life in victory over sin and death and hell. He now reigns as Lord in heaven and will one day return to be with all those who believe in him, forever. Whoever believes in Jesus Christ and accepts him in faith will be saved. They will belong to Christ, receive the Holy Spirit, and have eternal life.

> For it is by grace you have been saved, through faith – and this is not from yourselves, it is the gift of God – not by works, so that no one can boast.
> *Ephesians 2:8–9*

So what makes a person a Christian?

A person becomes a Christian by entering into a relationship with God through *faith* in the person of Jesus Christ. Faith means believing *and* trusting. You cannot save yourself, but you can allow God to save you. It does not depend on what you do, but on what Jesus Christ has already done. Your only option is to receive salvation as a gift. There is no other way.

Becoming a Christian involves coming to God and admitting, without any excuses, that you have gone against him. It means

> if you declare with your mouth, 'Jesus is Lord,' and believe in your heart that God raised him from the dead, you will be saved.
> *Romans 10:9*

admitting that you need to be forgiven and need his help to live a changed life. It involves humbly recognising that you cannot save yourself but need God to save you. It means making a decision to believe in Jesus Christ – to place your trust in what he has done for you, to accept him as God's sacrifice in your place – and allowing him to save you. It involves actually taking the step of asking for and receiving God's forgiveness, and inviting Jesus Christ to enter your life through the presence of the Holy Spirit. It also means making a decision to set out in a new direction, to live a different life; to live God's way to please him instead of living your own way to please yourself.

What makes a person a Christian is *faith*, believing in Jesus Christ, allowing him to save you from all your past failings, trusting in him, depending on him and agreeing to follow his way of living.

What *does* make a person a Christian:

> Very truly I tell you, whoever hears my word and believes him who sent me has eternal life and will not be judged but has crossed over from death to life.
> John 5:24

- **Admitting** that you have messed up by going against God and need his help
- **Deciding** to believe in Jesus Christ and trust him to save you from this mess
- **Asking** him to forgive you and enter into your life
- **Agreeing** to live God's way instead of your own

In chapter 4 we will look more closely at 'Starting a Relationship with God', but first, we will consider some of the stumbling blocks that can get in the way.

3

Ten Stumbling Blocks

The Christian message is God speaking to us. Each of us will respond differently to this message because we are all individuals. We think differently and we react differently. How we respond is not simply a matter of what we know or the level of our understanding; it is also a matter of how we *feel* about it and the personal experiences we have had. It is not human nature to look at things in a completely detached and analytical way. We think about things and have feelings about them all at the same time – the two intertwine. This is how God made us and he communicates with us in both of these ways: through the intellect of our minds and through the inner senses of our hearts.

There is, however, a danger in this. The danger is that we let our hearts rule our heads. If we do this, we will hear only what we want to hear; we will believe the things

> God is not human, that he should lie, not a human being, that he should change his mind. Does he speak and then not act? Does he promise and not fulfil?
> Numbers 23:19

that we like the sound of and become strangely deaf to the things that make us uncomfortable. In this way we can start to make up our own version of the truth. We begin to conceive our own version of reality and then convince ourselves we are right. Christians, however, believe that truth is not something we make up to suit ourselves depending on our own opinions and preferences. Christians believe that *absolute* truth exists, the truth that comes from God. God's truth is the same for every single person; it is not one thing to one person and something different to someone else. God's truth is completely constant, it does not change with time; it is the same yesterday, today and forever. God's truth is therefore totally dependable.

> As the heavens are higher than the earth, so are my ways higher than your ways and my thoughts than your thoughts.
> Isaiah 55:9

We may be troubled by many important questions; about our world, about life or about ourselves. Often we are unable to make any sense of things. However, God can make sense of them and he will help us to if we let him. God knows all the answers to every question. He and he alone understands all things because he made everything and rules over all creation. We clearly do not understand everything and this is because we are limited. We are limited by our capacity to understand things that are far above us. We are also limited to the extent that God chooses to reveal things to us. So when it comes to the complex issues of this world and our personal lives, God has perfect answers to all our questions, but we are not necessarily able to fully grasp hold of them.

Understanding can be hard to find; however, there is an

approach that can guide us as we wrestle to find the answers. That is to consider things in the light of what we know about God. We can base our answers on our understanding of who God is, what he is like and his purposes for the human race. God is our Almighty Creator; he is perfect, holy, just, loving, merciful and kind. He passionately wants to save every single person from all that has gone wrong in their lives and in the world around us. He is the God that heals, restores, reconciles and mends. The answers God would give us will always be completely consistent with his divine character.

Finding peace in the face of troubling questions can never simply be a matter of persuading the mind. God is the living God who wants to touch our whole lives. We will only begin to find peace when we allow him to speak to our hearts as well as our minds. To do that, we need to take the risk of believing in him and trusting him.

1. I CAN'T BELIEVE GOD EXISTS

God is spirit and we cannot see him. For some, this presents a real problem: how can we believe in a God we cannot see? In fact there are many things we cannot see, such as the electromagnetic waves emanating from a mobile phone, but we still believe in their existence because we experience the effect they have. So it is with God; we cannot see God, but we can see evidence of him. God reveals himself to us through creation. We are born into an amazing world and if we make the effort to look past the mess we have made of

> For since the creation of the world God's invisible qualities – his eternal power and divine nature – have been clearly seen, being understood from what has been made, so that people are without excuse.
> Romans 1:20

it we will see glimpses of its true glory. The natural world is awesome in its grandeur and power. It is enchanting in its intricate beauty. It is captivating in its intensity and variety of life. Whether in dramatic mountain scenery, a beautiful scented garden, or in the delightful innocence of a young child's smile, we may, for just a moment, connect with the deeper significance of creation. Through these things God speaks to us. He is saying that the world is not just accidental; it is designed. The world did not just happen; it was created. The world does not progress randomly; it is under control. God is the Creator and he reveals himself to us through what he has made. Creation reflects something of the image of the one who made it, and when we gaze at that reflection we see something of God himself. It perhaps takes more 'faith' to believe creation 'just happened' and continues on automatic pilot than to believe that there is a loving and powerful Creator and Ruler behind it all.

> 'Are you the one ...?' Jesus replied, 'Go back and report to John what you hear and see: the blind receive sight, the lame walk, those who have leprosy are cleansed, the deaf hear, the dead are raised, and the good news is proclaimed to the poor.'
> Matthew 11:3–5

Although we cannot see God today, the world was given a miraculous opportunity to meet God at first hand. God revealed himself in the person of Jesus Christ. Jesus claimed to be God. The truth of this claim was demonstrated by the miracles he performed and his resurrection back to life. The amazing life of Jesus is very well recorded and documented, not only in the Bible but also in thousands of independent manuscripts. The teaching, miracles, death and resurrection of Christ are historical facts. Many sceptical academic scholars have diligently studied the history of Christ, meaning to disprove Christian claims. However, they have been so overwhelmed by the weight of the supporting evidence that they have been forced to conclude that the Christian message must be true and have become Christians themselves.

The outward evidence of creation and the history of Jesus are powerful witnesses to the truth of God's existence. However, perhaps most compelling of all is the internal witness of our own spirituality. We were made to live in a relationship with God; without this relationship we are incomplete. We have deep spiritual needs and if we deny these needs we are left with a sense of emptiness. People go to great lengths to fill this emptiness with whatever the world has to offer, but they rarely seem to realise that they are simply pursuing poor substitutes for the real thing – God himself. The evidence of God's existence is in us from birth. It is evident in our in-built instinctive knowledge of God's will, our conscience that enables us to tell right from wrong. Most critically, it is evident in our deep inner longings to be loved, to be significant, and to be understood.

> the requirements of the law are written on their hearts, their consciences also bearing witness
> *Romans 2:15*

> But if ... you seek the LORD your God, you will find him if you seek him with all your heart and with all your soul.
> *Deuteronomy 4:29*

For those who have taken the step of faith and become Christians there is one overwhelming reason why they are sure God exists: because they know him. Christians experience a real personal relationship with the living God. His presence in their lives is a constant and powerful assurance that what they believe is true. They know him and love him, and they experience his love and care acting in their lives.

There is abundant evidence of the reality of God's existence if you are willing to open your eyes and heart to receive it. You can choose to ignore God, but it is hard to deny his existence. You may decide to reject him, but he still loves you and wants you to know him. You have a spiritual dimension; if you open yourself up to God, and earnestly seek him, you will find him.

2. I'M NOT INTERESTED IN RELIGION

'Religion' – the word alone is often enough to put some people right off anything to do with Christianity. It can be so contentious; religion seems to have caused so much conflict in the world. Alternatively, it may arouse thoughts of drab old buildings or dull and dreary services. It may evoke images of tedious ceremonies and incomprehensible rituals. Religion seems to be out of touch with the 'real' world and to have lost its relevance to the high-energy, high-tech modern society we now live in. It appears to consist of a long list of do's and don'ts designed to restrict people's freedom to enjoy themselves and generally make life a little miserable.

> If you hold to my teaching, you are really my disciples. Then you will know the truth, and the truth will set you free.
> John 8:31–32

In fact, Christianity is not centred on a church building but on a person. It is not all about rules but about a relationship. It does not stifle joy but offers freedom to discover and experience true joy. Christianity is about a real and meaningful relationship with someone extraordinary, God himself. It is difficult to imagine what could be more exciting and fulfilling than being in a relationship with the amazing God who made us. He is fearfully powerful, yet gentle and loving. He is vast and overwhelming, yet intimate and sensitive. He is glorious and majestic, yet humble and serving. Jesus Christ invites everyone to enter into a relationship with God. Jesus offers everyone the opportunity to experience true freedom. Jesus sets people free from the enslaving effects of wrong behaviours that lead into disappointment and emptiness. Jesus gives people freedom to know God and experience deeper meaning and purpose.

> Whoever loves money never has enough; whoever loves wealth is never satisfied with their income. This too is meaningless.
> *Ecclesiastes 5:10*

Some people think more deeply about things than others, but at some time or other most people question what life is really all about. Very few people honestly claim to be fully satisfied by the things the world has to offer. No matter what they gain, no matter how successful they become, no matter what pleasures they pursue, they do not find true happiness. The promises of the world are alluring, but hollow. However much they have, it is not quite enough. The deeper they indulge in something, the less gratifying it becomes and they need something more. The lure of worldly happiness always lies just out of reach. If anyone is brave enough to pause and ask 'Is this it?' they are unlikely to find any real answers or much comfort. They are left with no option but to just keep on going, resigned to making the most of it despite so many unfulfilled longings inside.

> I have come that they may have life, and have it to the full.
> John 10:10

The truth is that there *is* more to life, much more. There is true life in God, there is eternity. Christianity, when it is as God intends it to be, is not dull, restrictive or pointless. It is the most rewarding, fulfilling and meaningful life that any person can have. It is life in all its fullness, freedom of life as it is given by God, life with a guaranteed joyful future that lasts forever. If the Christian message is true then it is life *without* God that is pointless.

> Christ loved us and gave himself up for us as a fragrant offering and sacrifice to God.
> Ephesians 5:2

You may say that you are not interested in God, but he is intensely interested in you; he knows absolutely everything about you, every detail of your hopes and dreams, desires and needs. He deeply loves you, and your disinterest hurts him. He loves you so much that he gave Jesus to die for you. Jesus offers you the option of true life with real freedom and an eternal future of blessing in heaven.

3. IT'S OKAY FOR YOU BUT IT'S NOT FOR ME

We live in a very consumer-orientated world. Never before have so many people had so much choice. So much so that advertising is constantly spurred on to ever greater lengths to grab our attention in order to persuade, seduce, allure and entice us. There are so many competing voices striving to get us to listen. At the same time we have become ever increasingly individualistic. We make our own very individual choices, we do our own very individual thing and it does not seem to matter what everyone else does. You can do whatever you want and believe whatever you like, so long as it does not harm anyone. If you have the resources it is possible to demand almost anything you want. You can create your recipe for life, choose 'one of these' and 'one of those', 'a piece of this' and 'a bit of that', to suit your own personal preferences.

This is the attitude that many people bring to the matter of Christianity. They do not mind if someone else is a Christian, but it does not suit them to be one. Or at least it does not suit them right now, but who knows, perhaps it will later on. Or perhaps they choose to embrace a Christian idea or two, or accept a selection of its more attractive moral ethics, but reject everything else. Christianity to them is simply another option. Something to pick and choose from out of the bewildering array of choices that confront them. Something to opt for if they happen to fancy it, or if they think it just might work for them when the need arises.

Unfortunately, people who think like this have not actually understood the Christian message. Christianity claims to be about truth, not just *a* truth or *some* truth but *the* truth, the absolute truth that comes from God. God's truth is that he exists, that he made us, that he loves us and desires eternal happiness for us. However, there is a serious problem. The problem is that we are separated from him

> For the time will come when people will not put up with sound doctrine. Instead, to suit their own desires, they will gather round them a great number of teachers to say what their itching ears want to hear. They will turn their ears away from the truth and turn aside to myths.
> 2 Timothy 4:3–4

> Whoever believes in him is not condemned, but whoever does not believe stands condemned already because they have not believed in the name of God's one and only Son.
> John 3:18

by all the wrong in our lives. We are answerable to him for our failures; we need forgiveness and to be saved from the consequences. God's truth is that everyone has a desperate need to be brought back into a relationship with him by believing in Jesus Christ.

> Whoever believes in the Son has eternal life, but whoever rejects the Son will not see life, for God's wrath remains on them.
> John 3:36

Christianity is not merely a harmless option that does not really matter. It's not just something for the few it happens to suit. Either it's true or it's not. Either it's for everybody or it's for nobody. If it's *not* true then Christians are sadly deluded people and they are wasting their time. If it *is* true then every single person alive must face the consequences of the choice they make about God. Everyone makes a choice about God, whether it is made deliberately and consciously or simply by default. You have the straightforward choice, either to believe God's truth and accept him, or to deny his truth and reject him; there is no middle road.

4. IT DOESN'T WORK, I'VE TRIED IT BEFORE

> As for God, his way is perfect: the LORD's word is flawless.
> 2 Samuel 22:31

Many people have had some sort of experience of Christianity at one time or another. Unfortunately this experience may not necessarily have been a positive one. Whatever the nature of the problem, it may have been significant enough to cause them to fall away from their Christian faith, feeling bored, disappointed or hurt. Something somewhere along the way has obviously gone wrong. God himself claims to be perfect, and if this is true then it means it is impossible for him to ever let anyone down. So where does the problem lie?

Some people are deeply disappointed with church. Perhaps they found it to be dull and rather depressing. Feeling dry and bored, they seek fulfilment elsewhere. Or perhaps they found the teaching and activities to be lacking in real relevance. Unable to grasp the point of it all, they soon drift away. Still others might have been let down by fellow Christians or church leaders whose attitude was not all it should have been. Feeling hurt and resentful, they walk out.

Unfortunately we live in a world that is imperfect. Every one of us, Christian or not, has been spoiled by all the wrong things that have infiltrated our lives. Therefore, whilst God is perfect, no-one else is. Every single person has shortcomings; everyone makes mistakes. Consequently, churches can be dull and Christians hurt each other. Christians ought to reflect the character of God, but it is a mistake to judge God solely based on the behaviour of his people. God is supreme and alone as God; no-one is like him, not even remotely close. Churches are not full of perfect saints. They are full of imperfect people who have begun to realise just how desperately they need God, a group of real people making faltering steps towards him. To see God in his true glory we need to learn to look past human failings.

Others give up on their belief because the Christian life turns out to be harder than they thought it would be. They expected life to be easy, but it proves to be a struggle. They hoped that everything would suddenly fall neatly into place and that difficulties would disappear. However, they soon discover that God's way of doing things is different from theirs. There are new challenges to face – battles against temptation, opposition from unbelievers – and sacrifices are called for.

The Christian life can be rich and rewarding, but it is not the easy option. God does not promise Christians a trouble-free life, but he does promise to take them through their troubles. If we are to live under God's blessing then we must get the foundations right. An interest in the 'things of God' is good, but what God actually asks us for is a genuine wholehearted decision to give our lives to him. A half-hearted commitment to God will not make us strong enough to stand up against the worries, temptations and troubles of life. Our relationship with God will only really work if we are prepared to completely trust him and depend on him. Living by depending on our own strength, or living a kind of double life, will only lead to inner tension and anguish.

> Some people ... hear the word and at once receive it with joy. But since they have no root, they last only a short time. When trouble or persecution comes ... they quickly fall away. Still others ... hear the word; but the worries of this life, the deceitfulness of wealth and the desires for other things come in and choke the word.
> Mark 4:15–19

> Taste and see that the LORD is good; blessed is the one who takes refuge in him.
> Psalm 34:8

Whatever may have gone wrong in the past, it does not mean that the Christian message is untrue. However, it does mean that people who feel let down by Christianity have not entered into the full blessing God has for them. The failings of others in church can be very hurtful and the struggles of life can be very discouraging. However, Christianity is not centred on church and it does not depend on how well we cope. Christianity is centred on a relationship with God, and it depends on what Jesus Christ has already done for us. Any Christian who does not recognise these truths, or loses sight of them, is bound to suffer heartache. God asks us to make a wholehearted decision to place our faith in him, regardless or our circumstances and regardless of past experiences.

He also asks us to truly depend on him and to persevere when our faith is tested.

> Though the mountains be shaken and the hills be removed, yet my unfailing love for you will not be shaken.
> Isaiah 54:10

God is utterly dependable, he is faithful and true, he is completely fair and he does not make mistakes. His love for you is unconditional, wholehearted and everlasting. If you step towards God in faith, he will meet you; this is his promise. If you commit to him, *he* will not let you down, no matter what happens.

5. DON'T WORRY, I'M ALRIGHT

Some of us set relatively high standards for ourselves whilst others are much more self-lenient. Personal standards may well vary from one person to the next, but we all have them. These standards form the basis of the decisions we make about how to live our lives. Some people are shining examples to all of us. Always so caring and kind, they seem to have time for everyone. Unselfishly they devote themselves to helping others. Even when they have good cause to complain, they are constantly cheerful. Others simply pride themselves on being decent and honest people. They treat everyone with respect and stay well away from trouble. Many people would describe themselves as good people, although they would readily admit to not being a saint. 'I may not be perfect, but I'm not a bad person.' Perhaps they would call themselves a 'good Christian', because they believe that being good is what makes you one, although this is actually not true.

> Do not deceive yourselves. If any of you think you are wise by the standards of this age, you should become 'fools' so that you may become wise. For the wisdom of this world is foolishness in God's sight.
> 1 Corinthians 3:18–19

The problem with human standards is that they are likely to change over time and with differing circumstances. They are prone to inconsistency from one person to the next. For example, people's perspectives tend to change as they get older and become more widely experienced. Wisdom comes with time, and views on some of the complex issues of the day are likely to mellow from the more black-and-white opinions that they might once have held. For others, their views may change with the events in their lives. Previously they may have been quick to pass judgement, but later their perspective is altered when it 'happens to them'.

> Indeed, there is no one on earth who is righteous, no one who does what is right and never sins.
> Ecclesiastes 7:20

Underlying these views is the fundamental belief that everything is relative. People tend to judge themselves by comparing themselves with other people, and reckon that they are doing alright. If they claim to believe in God and life after death, they are also likely to believe that they should probably get into heaven okay. They may reason that when the time eventually comes for them to meet God he will look kindly on them and say, 'Well, I suppose you've lived a fairly good life. You'll do – come on in!' Unfortunately this is not true; he can't.

TEN STUMBLING BLOCKS

> Therefore no one will be declared righteous in God's sight by the works of the law; rather, through the law we become conscious of our sin. But now apart from the law the righteousness of God has been made known ... This righteousness is given through faith in Jesus Christ to all who believe.
> *Romans 3:20–22*

The problem is that our standards and God's standards are radically different. We tend to compare ourselves with others and conclude that we are not that bad. We can usually find someone else who, in our own opinion, is worse than we are. We are quick to detect other people's faults and are equally quick to come up with some very good reasons why we should be excused our own failings. God on the other hand uses a different measure. He compares us with his standard of complete perfection and concludes that everyone falls well short.

No matter how good we are, or how hard we try, we cannot get into heaven by living a good life. Our lives are simply never going to be good enough. The pass mark is perfection and no-one makes the grade. God, however, has provided a way for us to be saved from all our failings forever. He has made it possible for everyone to be saved from his judgement and enter heaven instead. He has made it possible for us to be absolutely certain about it.

> But blessed is the one who trusts in the LORD, whose confidence is in him.
> *Jeremiah 17:7*

You are only 'alright' if you have decided to believe in Jesus Christ and trust him as the only one who can save you. If you *have* done this then you will be able to face God with absolute confidence. If you have *not* done this then you have no basis for any confidence at all. You cannot save yourself; you need a Saviour.

6. HOW CAN A LOVING GOD SEND PEOPLE TO HELL?

God's love for each one of us is so deep that he aches for us to live in a relationship with him. His mercy is so great that he longs to forgive us for every wrong, no matter how awful, no matter how persistent and unrepentant we may have been in the past. So if God has so much compassion towards everyone, how can he allow anyone to go to hell? How can there even be such a thing or place as hell in the first place?

This subject is as difficult for Bible-believing Christians as it is for anyone else. There is uncertainty over the precise nature of eternity. This applies to the attractive parts about heaven and the new earth, as well as the unpleasant parts about hell. Therefore, there are various views on how the teachings of the Bible should be interpreted. Nevertheless, the Bible does make it clear that at some point in the future, at the end of history, Christ will return. He will judge those who are still alive as well as those who have already died and he will finally complete God's plan to rid his world of all that is wrong and evil. So how will God go about putting the world right? To begin to get to grips with this question we first need to understand what the problem is.

At the very heart of our problem lies an important aspect of our God-given human nature. When God created us he gave us something very special; he gave us free will. Without this gift it would be impossible for us to truly love God. True love needs to be freely given. Therefore God gave us free will so that we could choose to return his love. He could easily have made us like computers, programmed to behave exactly the way he wanted. If he had done this then we would never have failed to go through the motions of perfect obedience. However, this would not have been a relationship of love but rather one of master and slave. Without free will, our acts of love would have been hollow and meaningless.

The tragedy lies in what the world has done with this free will: it has chosen to reject God and live in disobedience to him, to live its own way instead of his.

> But because of your stubbornness and your unrepentant heart, you are storing up wrath against yourself for the day of God's wrath, when his righteous judgement will be revealed.
> Romans 2:5

This is what God calls sin. Every single one of us is guilty of doing wrong and there are serious consequences for us if it is not dealt with. God is a God of great love and mercy, but he is also a God of holiness and justice.

> Yes, Lord God Almighty, true and just are your judgments.
> Revelation 16:7

God's holiness means that he cannot be intimately united with anyone who remains tainted. Sin spoils and it corrupts, but God is pure and must remain pure. Any compromise, however small, would corrupt the future perfection he has planned for those who choose him. Therefore, ultimately, at the end of this age, a final separation must take place. No imperfection can be allowed to enter the new creation God has planned, or it would be spoiled. Everything that remains corrupted needs to be separated; it needs to be excluded. This is what 'hell' actually is. It is an eternal existence utterly separated from God's life and love and goodness. This is the judgement of a holy God on sin, and there can be no alternative; the problem must be dealt with.

If we allow God to deal with all our mistakes and failures and take them from us, we are made clean. We are no longer contaminated but are made holy through Jesus

> For the message of the cross is foolishness to those who are perishing, but to us who are being saved it is the power of God.
>
> 1 Corinthians 1:18

Christ. In this way it becomes possible for us to fully enter God's presence. If, however, we persist in refusing to be separated from our sin and continue to cling on to it, then there is no alternative. We must go along with it into the place of exclusion. It is the 'rubbish' of sin that God consigns to hell, but if anyone refuses to let go of it then they will sadly end up being sent along with the rubbish.

God's passionate desire is for each of us to accept him, receive his love, love him in

> They perish because they refused to love the truth and so be saved.
>
> 2 Thessalonians 2:10

return and be saved. God does not want anyone to go this way. The thought of losing a single person breaks his heart. We all have a choice, either to accept God and be saved, or reject him and suffer the penalty. The opportunity to be saved is open to everyone, without exception. All we have to do is respond.

7. HOW CAN I BELIEVE IN GOD WITH SO MUCH SUFFERING IN THE WORLD?

The existence of suffering is for some an almost insurmountable barrier to any belief in God. If God is really almighty then he obviously has the power to end it. If he truly loves everyone then he must desperately want to stop it. So what is the problem?

Suffering is something that personally affects all of us. The world is full of suffering and every single person experiences suffering in one form or another. Some people suffer very

TEN STUMBLING BLOCKS

> when I hoped for good, evil came; when I looked for light, then came darkness. The churning inside me never stops; days of suffering confront me.
> *Job 30:26–27*

intensely for very long periods of time. Others simply suffer the everyday hardships and disappointments of life. We may not all experience the very worst forms of tragedy ourselves, but we can certainly witness the horror of them as they impact the lives of others.

Suffering comes in many different shapes and sizes and some if it appears to be beyond our control. Devastating natural disasters, horrific accidents and cruel diseases inflict incomprehensible pain on so many. Such suffering is seemingly indiscriminate as it

> The LORD saw how great the wickedness of the human race had become on the earth, and that every inclination of the thoughts of the human heart was only evil all the time. The LORD regretted that he had made human beings on the earth, and his heart was deeply troubled.
> *Genesis 6:5–6*

destroys the lives of innocent, helpless and young victims. In contrast, other forms of suffering do seem to be preventable. Much suffering comes as a direct result of the deliberate wrong choices people make. Their selfish and malicious actions inflict suffering on others as well as on themselves. Whether it is on the grand scale of international events or simply a fleeting encounter between two individuals, there are so many things that people say and do to hurt each other. Equally, there is so much that they don't do to help others when they could. Discrimination, complacency and pure self-interest lead them to decline to do anything to alleviate other people's difficulties.

The presence of suffering in the world is bewildering and

traumatic. Its existence can seem impossible to explain. Yet it is right that we should wrestle with such an important issue and seek a better understanding of it, no matter how difficult this may seem.

> For the creation was subjected to frustration, not by its own choice, but by the will of the one who subjected it, in hope that the creation itself will be liberated from its bondage to decay and brought into the freedom and glory of the children of God.
> Romans 8:20–21

Why is there so much suffering in the world? Why is there any suffering at all?

The world is full of suffering but it is not meant to be this way. There was no suffering in the perfect world God originally made, but the world decided to go its own way, to disobey God and live outside his perfect will. With this act of rebellion sin entered the world and, along with sin, in came suffering. Sin is the introduction of imperfection and with imperfection comes frustration and pain.

The whole of creation has been spoiled. Everything that exists is flawed and every single person is imperfect. Natural disasters, disease, human error and the wrong actions of men and women spread suffering throughout the world. Every one of us does some wrong and in this way we contribute to the world's suffering. Every single person's shortcomings hurt someone. Our actions may be downright deliberate or just an unwitting mistake. They can impact directly or indirectly. They affect the innocent as well as the guilty. We may hurt ourselves or someone else. The effect may be immediate or delayed. Whatever form it takes, disobedience to God's way of living is always ultimately destructive. The reason there is suffering in the world is because sin has entered it and made it imperfect. Suffering exists because we have rejected God.

Why does God not put an end to suffering? Why does he allow it to continue?

God is the all-powerful Creator who rules over the whole world. He is also the loving God who deeply desires the very best for everyone. God hates suffering, so why does he not do something about it?

The truth is that God *has* done something about suffering. He has begun to work out his perfect plan to rescue the world from its predicament. It was people's actions, not God's, that introduced suffering and evil into the world. However, God has not abandoned us to our own mess; in his great love and mercy he holds out the way of escape. God the Father sent Jesus Christ his Son into the world to save us. Through him, God has opened up the way for us to be saved from suffering forever.

Everyone who believes in Jesus Christ will one day enter the perfection of heaven. The spoiled world will be renewed and made perfect as it always should have been. There will be a new heaven and a new earth. All suffering

> Look! God's dwelling-place is now among the people, and he will dwell with them. They will be his people, and God himself will be with them and be their God. 'He will wipe every tear from their eyes. There will be no more death' or mourning or crying or pain, for the old order of things has passed away.
> *Revelation 21:3–4*

will come to a complete end; there will be no more pain, no more sadness and no more death. Every wrong will be put right and every injustice overturned. Every believer in Jesus will be completely healed and restored and will live with God in perfect happiness forever. All suffering and evil will be excluded from the new perfection that God will create. This is the amazing hope that God offers to us.

If God has a plan to rid the world of suffering, why does he not do it now? Why has he not done it already?

> with the Lord a day is like a thousand years, and a thousand years are like a day. The Lord is not slow in keeping his promise, as some understand slowness. Instead he is patient with you, not wanting anyone to perish, but everyone to come to repentance.
>
> 2 Peter 3:8–9

There was no suffering in the perfect world God created before the world rejected him. Neither will there be any suffering for those who spend eternity with him. Between these two end-points in history lies the mess of sin. Sin always leads to suffering; they are the inseparable twins. God cannot wipe away suffering without also wiping away everything imperfect. God's plan to save the world is therefore very radical. He must first purge it of everything that is corrupted and then make it anew. God plans to bring an end to the spoiled world we live in and then recreate it in order to restore perfection.

The problem is that only those who have allowed Jesus to clean them up from their failures and shortcomings can enter God's new creation. Everyone else faces alienation from God's goodness. God does not want anyone to be lost. He deeply loves every single person and wants each one to turn to him and be saved. Therefore he is very patient, waiting with great longing for as many as are willing to recognise the truth and change their minds about him. God's timing is perfect and he has appointed the right time for the new beginning. Jesus has promised to return and when the appointed time arrives he will certainly come. Then a wonderful new beginning will dawn for those who are ready to meet God.

The promise of future happiness is all very well, but where is God right now? Where is God when it really hurts?

> Praise be to the God and Father of our Lord Jesus Christ, the Father of compassion and the God of all comfort, who comforts us in all our troubles
> 2 Corinthians 1:3–4

Some people think that God is very distant and remote from their troubles, apparently unaware, uncaring and unfeeling. The truth is that he knows every minute detail of our experiences and he cares more deeply about us than we could ever imagine. The problem is that people prefer to keep God at a distance. They shy away from entering into a close relationship with him and so they do not actually know him. God loves each one of us passionately; he made us and we are all extremely precious to him. When we are hurt he is hurt and he longs for us to turn to him for healing. However, if we are to experience God's love and compassion we must come to him. We need to be prepared to turn to him and ask him for his help. Where is God when we are hurting? The answer is that he can be very, very close, as close as we are willing to allow him.

> Surely he took up our pain and bore our suffering, yet we considered him punished by God, stricken by him, and afflicted. But he was pierced for our transgressions, he was crushed for our iniquities; the punishment that brought us peace was on him, and by his wounds we are healed.
> Isaiah 53:4–5

God loves us so deeply that he is willing to share our suffering with us. God knows about suffering from first-

GOD'S LOVE AND TRUTH

hand experience. What can compare with the suffering Jesus went through for each one of us? Jesus Christ, God's only Son, took the heartbreak of all the wrong and evil of the world on himself and died a cruel, humiliating and painful death on a cross. God understands. If we let him, he will enter into our suffering with us and give us his help and strength. In the midst of our turmoil and pain he offers to bring us his comfort and peace. He will bear our burdens with us and share our pain. God may not instantly remove all our troubles, but he will give us his power and take us through them. We will be held firmly in the loving arms of the Almighty and kept eternally safe. We will discover that God is in control.

> Cast all your anxiety on him because he cares for you.
> 1 Peter 5:7

In the midst of our suffering God calls us to trust him and place our faith in him. He asks us to do this, not despite our suffering, but because of it. Suffering exists because the world has rejected God. Instead of accusing God we need to say sorry for our own part in it and turn to him for healing.

Suffering and evil are powerful witnesses to the fact that there is something dreadfully wrong with the world. This should lead you to ask, 'What has gone wrong?' and 'Why?' and 'What should I do?' Rather than blaming God and turning away from him, God wants you to turn towards him and trust him, to accept his help and strength, to receive his

> The LORD is righteous in all his ways and faithful in all he does. The LORD is near to all who call on him, to all who call on him in truth. He fulfils the desires of those who fear him; he hears their cry and saves them. The LORD watches over all who love him, but all the wicked he will destroy.
> Psalm 145:17–20

comfort and peace, to experience his love and compassion, to ask his forgiveness and to accept his offer of eternal happiness in heaven.

8. I DON'T THINK IT REALLY MATTERS WHICH RELIGION YOU FOLLOW

There are many different religions in the world and the wide array can seem baffling. Emerging new spiritual movements jostle alongside the great world religions rooted in ancient history. To make matters yet more complicated, many religions are subdivided into numerous smaller groups. Despite all the diversity, however, it is often possible to identify underlying similarities between the different sets of beliefs. It is hardly surprising therefore that when faced with such complexity some people are tempted to sweep aside the differences and conclude that all religions are basically the same. Perhaps they conclude that the differences between religious are simply a reflection of the various customs and practices that stem from different national cultures and histories.

It is certainly true that many religions do appear to have a number of things in common. For example: a belief in a spiritual world, a desire for life after death, a definition of how we ought to live, and a commitment to then living that way. There are also apparently similar goals. For example: to escape our present troubled existence, to enter into eternal happiness, and to achieve a state of peace with 'God'. If all religions really were basically the same then it would not matter which one you decided to follow. All you would need to do is choose a set of beliefs that appeals to you, remain true to them and then hope that everything works out for the best.

> So God created mankind in his own image, in the image of God he created them; male and female he created them.
> Genesis 1:27

The truth is that there is indeed an underlying common factor that accounts for the similarities between religions. The common factor is in our make-up: we have been created with a spiritual dimension. Inside each of us there is a fundamental need for the God who made us. God made us to live in a relationship with him and he has given us a basic desire for spiritual fulfilment, a desire that can only be truly fulfilled in him. Down through the ages this inner longing has inspired men and women to search, and this search has led people in many different directions. All religions are fuelled by the same deep yearning. We should therefore not be surprised that there are many common features between them.

> Jesus answered, 'I am the way and the truth and the life. No one comes to the Father except through me.'
> John 14:6

Christianity, however, makes a startling claim. It does not just claim to be one way to God, or simply the best way; it claims to be the *only* way. Christianity is absolutely unique. It is set apart from all other faiths by the person of Jesus Christ.

> For there is one God and one mediator between God and mankind, the man Christ Jesus, who gave himself as a ransom for all people.
> 1 Timothy 2:5–6

We all face a fundamental problem. None of us can ever be good enough to enter heaven by our own efforts. No matter how hard we try to live a good life, no matter how strict our discipline or how great our spiritual achievements, we will never make the grade of God's utter perfection. We are stuck with the fact that we cannot cure our own condition. We are imperfect, we are spoiled by our faults and failings, and it is impossible for us to make ourselves clean. We have a single desperate need: we need someone to save us. We need someone to do for us what we can never do for ourselves. We need Jesus Christ. Jesus is a completely unique person. Jesus is the perfect Son of God sent into the world by God the Father to deal with our guilt for us. Jesus took all our guilt on himself and died for us in our place to make us clean. Jesus is the one who was raised to life again in victory over sin and death and hell. Jesus Christ is the only one who can save us from our predicament. Without Jesus, we are left floundering in our own helplessness, grasping at what is out of reach, longing for something we can never have.

Many people live in hope, but their hope is nothing more than wishful thinking. They can never be certain about their eternal future because their religious beliefs dictate that their destiny is dependent upon themselves; on whether they are good enough or not. Christian hope is very different. Christians have a Saviour who is himself God, a living Lord who reigns in heaven. Christians are absolutely certain about their future. They are certain because it does not depend on what they do, but on what Jesus Christ has already done. They are certain because Jesus is not dead; he is alive.

> He is not here; he has risen, just as he said. Come and see the place where he lay. Then go quickly and tell his disciples: 'He has risen from the dead'
>
> Matthew 28:6–7

You can never lift yourself up to God; it is an impossible task and your best efforts are doomed to failure. God's amazing message is that you do not have to get up to him because he has come down to you. Jesus Christ came down to meet you

> Salvation is found in no one else, for there is no other name under heaven given to mankind by which we must be saved.
> Acts 4:12

where you are in all your need; he came to rescue you. Jesus is the only way to God. There is no other way you can be saved, only through Jesus Christ.

9. I'M NOT GOOD ENOUGH TO BE A CHRISTIAN

Some people consider themselves too unworthy of God to risk getting close to him.

> The Lord our God is merciful and forgiving, even though we have rebelled against him
> Daniel 9:9

They believe that they are in too much of a mess to become involved in something like Christianity. They reckon that they have too many ugly problems lurking in the dark corners of their lives and so they stay away from God for fear of being made to feel guilty and ashamed. If they were ever to let God get any nearer, they would feel a need to get their lives sorted out first. They would want to feel better in themselves, more presentable, more able to stand in his holy presence without feeling quite so ashamed. They cannot believe that God would want them as they are.

> For God did not send his Son into the world to condemn the world, but to save the world through him.
> John 3:17

The surprising truth is that this is exactly how God wants us to come to him, just as we are. No-one is worthy of God, no matter how righteous they might appear. It is impossible for anyone to ever be good enough to deserve God. If it had been possible then there would have been no need for Jesus Christ to enter the world and die for us. Every single person, without exception, has faults and failings and falls way short of God's perfect standard. Everyone needs to receive God's forgiveness and be saved; we are all in the same predicament.

The way to get our lives sorted out is to allow God to do the sorting. The way to get cleaned up is to let God do the cleaning. Jesus did not come into the world to condemn it, but to save it. He did not come to heal those who are well, but those who are sick. It is not those who are self-assured and full of self-confidence that find God, rather it is those who recognise how desperately they need him. It is not those who help themselves that are saved; it is those who allow God to rescue them.

> Jesus answered them, 'It is not the healthy who need a doctor, but those who are ill. I have not come to call the righteous, but sinners to repentance.'
> Luke 5:31–32

Although we can never be worthy of God, we are of infinite worth to him. In his loving eyes we are of incredible value. The depth of God's love for us is beyond our comprehension. We can pretend to hide things from him, but it is impossible to deceive him; he knows absolutely everything about us. God knows us so intimately that he even knows the exact number of hairs on our head. He also knows our every weakness and failing and yet he loves us so much that he gave up Jesus to die for us. This is the God of such great love that we can approach him with complete confidence that he will joyfully welcome us. We can come to him with confidence, not because of our own righteousness, but because of his amazing grace.

> I pray that you ... may... grasp how wide and long and high and deep is the love of Christ, and to know this love that surpasses knowledge – that you may be filled to the measure of all the fullness of God.
> Ephesians 3:17–19

> Truly I tell you, anyone who will not receive the kingdom of God like a little child will never enter it.
> Mark 10:15

God asks us to open up to him with childlike trust and stop pretending. He wants us to lay everything before him as it really is and to throw ourselves unreservedly on his unfailing goodness. God deeply loves every single one of us. He longs to enter into our lives, bringing his healing and wholeness. He wants to free us from the pain that has come through past hurts and failures. He is the God of kindness and mercy who forgives and restores.

No matter who you are, no matter what you have done, God's great love for you will never diminish. He is the God of overwhelming goodness, mercy and compassion. He longs for you to turn to him, to come to

> So he got up and went to his father. But while he was still a long way off, his father saw him and was filled with compassion for him; he ran to his son, threw his arms round him and kissed him.
> Luke 15:20

him honestly and humbly, without pretence. To come and ask him to heal, restore and forgive you. The way to come to God is just as you are. You are his deeply loved and long-lost child; he will open his arms wide and warmly embrace you.

10. NOW ISN'T THE RIGHT TIME

Some people are inwardly convinced that there is truth in the Christian message but do nothing about it. Deep inside they have perhaps begun to detect the voice of God gently calling them. A slight stirring takes place in their hearts and part of them feels drawn towards God. Yet something else in them squirms and shouts, 'NO!' That inner voice makes all sorts of objections and directs their attention towards every conceivable distraction. So they resist God. One day they will perhaps do something about the spiritual thoughts and feelings they have been experiencing, but not right now. Now is just not the right time.

For some, the issue centres on some of the 'pleasures' of the world. There are things in their lives that they know are at odds

> What good will it be for someone to gain the whole world, yet forfeit their soul?
> Matthew 16:26

with Christian beliefs, but they love them and do not want to give them up. They want the best of both worlds. They want to indulge their worldly desires now, but also to make sure that they will be alright in eternity, if it exists. Perhaps they reason that they can live however they please now, then cleverly convert to Christianity at the last minute. To them, Christianity is a kind of insurance policy, something you do just in case, at the last possible moment. However, as time passes, the pleasures they pursue become more and more hollow, and a nagging dissatisfaction sets in. Underneath it all, they know something is missing, but they have slowly become blind and insensitive to the harm the wrong things have been doing to their lives. A desire to change may emerge, but the habits of a lifetime prove very hard to break. Something inside them starts to say it is already too late.

> I denied myself nothing my eyes desired; I refused my heart no pleasure ... Yet when I surveyed all that my hands had done and what I had toiled to achieve, everything was meaningless, a chasing after the wind; nothing was gained under the sun.
> Ecclesiastes 2:10–11

Yet others are too concerned with what they want to achieve first. They are driven to attain their own goals in life, to set themselves up. When this is done they plan to sit back a bit and enjoy life, to reap the rewards for their efforts. Only then will they have time for things like Christianity. For now, they are far too busy. There is too much to do; they have other more important priorities. The problem is that the right time never comes. The list of things they want to achieve is never completed; the goalposts just keep on moving. They get older and older without recognising that they are really no nearer to the fulfilment and bliss they once dreamed of.

> Many are the plans in a person's heart, but it is the LORD's purpose that prevails.
> Proverbs 19:21

People who put God on hold are making some seriously wrong presumptions. They are in effect saying that they are in full control of their own lives and are the masters of their own destiny. However, Christians believe that it is God who is in control. The Almighty, the living God, the Creator of all things – he is the one who rules over all. The truth is that we are not in control. We do not know what will happen today, tomorrow or any time in the future. We do not know when we will die or how. We do not know what our circumstances will become or what freedom we will have to make decisions. We have a choice: either live at the mercy of a spoiled and unfair world, or place ourselves in the safe hands of the all-powerful God of love.

> 'For I know the plans I have for you,' declares the LORD, 'plans to prosper you and not to harm you, plans to give you hope and a future.'
> Jeremiah 29:11

Another wrong presumption is that life is better without God in the way. In other words, the belief that living a life of wrong is more desirable than living a right way of life. In effect, these people are saying that God has got it completely wrong. God claims that his way of living is best, so to reject his way is to call him a liar. Rather than believe God, they conclude that his way must be burdensome and dull, whereas the world's way must be exciting and fun.

The world's way may at times seem alluring and tempting, but it ultimately leads to heartache and pain.

> The god of this age has blinded the minds of unbelievers, so that they cannot see the light of the gospel that displays the glory of Christ
> 2 Corinthians 4:4

It leads to disappointment, discontentment, dissatisfaction, emptiness, frustration, inner tensions, resentment, bitterness and regret. The world is deceitful, and all too easily we fall for the lies. The truth is that God's way leads to blessing and wholeness. It leads to healing, release, freedom, peace, exciting discovery, fulfilment, joy, and a life full of real meaning and purpose. When someone becomes a Christian they are likely to have only one regret: 'Why have I wasted so much time?' 'Why didn't I do it sooner?'

> I tell you, now is the time of God's favour, now is the day of salvation.
> 2 Corinthians 6:2

If God is tugging at your heart you can either respond to him or resist him. If he is speaking to you about your life, you can listen to him or ignore him. He has given you the choice, but the right time is always now. Now is the time for you to become a Christian. It is now that you can make your eternal future certain. It is now that you can start to make the most of the rest of your life. Now is the time.

4

Starting a Relationship with God

BECOMING A CHRISTIAN – HOW IS IT DONE?

Becoming a Christian involves entering into a new relationship with God through faith in Jesus Christ. At one level Christianity

> 'Sirs, what must I do to be saved?'
> They replied, 'Believe in the Lord Jesus, and you will be saved'
> Acts 16:30–31

is as mysterious and as unfathomable as God himself. At another level it is simple enough for a young child to grasp. All that is needed is the most basic understanding of your need of God. Although Christianity can be relatively simple, it is life-changing. Therefore it can be a great challenge to take the apparently simple step of making a genuine commitment.

> the LORD your God is gracious and compassionate. He will not turn his face from you if you return to him.
> 2 Chronicles 30:9

If you are prepared to take that step then you can, right now. God is longing for you to do just that. Whoever you are, wherever

75

you are, whatever you have done or not done, whatever your present circumstances, God is there for you. If you come to him, he will joyfully receive you; that is his promise.

There is no set formula to follow, no rituals, no special jargon. It is not how well you understand, or the exact words you pray that really matter to God; it is the attitude of your heart. All you need do is speak to God with sincerity, perhaps using a prayer like the one at the end of this chapter. Maybe you know a Christian you could share this time with, if you want someone to help you. Or you can simply be quiet and alone with God; it's up to you.

To give you some more help, here are a few steps that you may find useful.

Knowledge

You need just some understanding of the Christian message; you must recognise that you need God. Here are the main points once again:

> Christ was sacrificed once to take away the sins of many; and he will appear a second time, not to bear sin, but to bring salvation to those who are waiting for him.
> *Hebrews 9:28*

- God loves you and wants you to live in a special relationship with him
- However, along with everyone else, you have fallen short in God's eyes, you have gone off track and done things that are wrong; we are all guilty
- God calls this 'sin', and its spoiling effect separates us from him
- If this problem is not dealt with, the consequences are awful: you will stay separated from God and will end up

being finally and completely cut off from his love and goodness forever; this is what hell is
- You need saving from this destiny, but are helpless to do it yourself
- In his mercy and out of love God has made it possible for you to be saved
- Jesus Christ came into the world to save you by dying in your place and taking all your guilt on himself
- Jesus Christ was raised to life in victory over death and offers you a fresh start and a new life
- Jesus will return to be with all those who believe in him; he will live with them in a renewed and perfect creation
- If you decide to believe in Jesus Christ and accept him in faith, you will be saved; you will receive the Holy Spirit and have eternal life

Faith

You need to decide to believe that these things are true and then decide to act on your belief, in faith. This involves an act of your will. It does

> This righteousness is given through faith in Jesus Christ to all who believe.
> Romans 3:22

not depend on feelings and emotions; you must simply *decide* to do it. Firstly, faith means believing. Secondly, it means setting about living a life that is consistent with what you believe. Faith combines these two elements, belief and action working together in harmony

- Decide to believe in Jesus Christ, put your faith and trust in him, and allow him to save you from all that is wrong in your life

- Decide to invite Jesus to come into your life and live with you through the presence of the Holy Spirit
- Decide to allow God to help you start living his way and stop doing the things you know are wrong
- Decide to start depending on God and trusting him with your life

Attitude

God is not interested in external appearances. He is interested in what is really in your heart. He knows you intimately; he knows absolutely everything about you. He knows the best and he knows the worst. There is no place for pretence or excuses, and there is no room for pride. He wants you to come to him just as you are, with openness and honesty. He deeply loves you and he looks on you with mercy and compassion. He sees you as you are now *and* as the person he wants to help you become. He is waiting for you to come to him. You need to come to God with the right attitude.

> 'God opposes the proud but shows favour to the humble.' Submit yourselves, then, to God.
> James 4:6–7

- Come to God with confidence, knowing that he deeply loves you and will accept you
- Be honest; recognise that you have wronged God and need him to forgive you and save you
- Be respectful; remember that he is the almighty and holy God who made you
- Come ready to say sorry, without excuses
- Come willing to yield to God, prepared to depend on him and trust him

STARTING A RELATIONSHIP WITH GOD

> Struggling with the question 'Is there really sin in my life?'
>
> Find a place where you can be quietly alone with God, unhurried and unpressured. Speak to God about it, ask him the question, then sit and think and see what comes to mind:
>
> God, if I really am guilty of sin then please show me ...

Action

You may have understood the Christian message. You may have decided that it is true. You may also genuinely feel moved by God. However, none of this is any good at all if you do not act on it. You need to actually take the step of becoming a Christian. You need to make a decision. Jesus only becomes your Saviour if you accept him.

> So I say to you: ask and it will be given to you; seek and you will find; knock and the door will be opened to you. For everyone who asks receives; the one who seeks finds; and to the one who knocks, the door will be opened.
> Luke 11:9–10

To take the step, you need to talk to God. Talking to God is called prayer. Use your own words to express yourself to him:

- Admit to God that you have gone wrong and lived your own way instead of his
- Admit that you need God to help you by saving you from this mess
- Ask him to forgive you, knowing that he will
- Tell him that you have decided to believe and trust in Jesus Christ
- Ask him to help you to start making changes and learning to live his way
- Ask Jesus to enter your life by his Spirit, right now

- Be confident that a dramatic change has just taken place and thank Jesus for this

Perhaps you would like to use the following prayer, or something similar in your own words.

> Dear God
> I'm sorry for living in a way that has hurt and offended you. Please forgive me. I want to change.
>
> Thank you, Jesus, for dying for me in the way you did, so that our relationship could be mended. I want our new relationship to begin right now.
>
> I want you to save me from the mess created by every wrong thing I have ever said, thought or done.
>
> Please enter my life now and live with me through your Holy Spirit, and help me to start living your way instead of mine.
> Amen

5

Living the Christian Life

I HAVE BECOME A CHRISTIAN – NOW WHAT?

If you come to God in faith, he will receive you; this is his promise. Therefore, if you have made a sincere and genuine commitment to him, you have

> Everyone who calls on the name of the Lord will be saved.
> Romans 10:13

become a Christian. You have entered into an exciting new relationship with him through Jesus Christ. It is God's gift to you and he has sealed it by giving you the Holy Spirit. Nothing can ever break your relationship with God again.

> For he has rescued us from the dominion of darkness and brought us into the kingdom of the Son he loves, in whom we have redemption, the forgiveness of sins.
> Colossians 1:13–14

A wonderful transition has taken place: your position before God has entirely changed. You were living with guilt and shame; now you have been forgiven and set free from it all. You were without hope; now you have inherited eternal life with God in heaven. Spiritually, you were like a dead person; now you have been brought to life. You were alienated from God; now he has adopted you into his family and calls you his son or daughter. You were bankrupt of eternal riches; now he has made you an heir, with Jesus Christ, of the Kingdom of Heaven!

> See what great love the Father has lavished on us, that we should be called children of God! ... what we will be has not yet been made known. But we know that when Christ appears, we shall be like him
> 1 John 3:1–2

As a Christian your life now has real meaning and purpose: to live in a fulfilling and loving relationship with your amazing Maker, to please him and to allow him to make you into the person he wants you to be. You also now have true direction: you are heading for a home in heaven. You have embarked upon an incredible journey with God, a journey that has a clear and wonderful destination. This is real life, life in all its fullness, life without the emptiness.

> I give them eternal life, and they shall never perish; no one will snatch them out of my hand.
> John 10:28

How do you feel? Your feelings may be hard to describe. Perhaps you feel a new peace and joy inside, perhaps also a sense of freedom and release. Or you may not feel much at all just yet. Whatever your emotions, it does not change God's truth; he keeps his promises. Know that you are saved, know that you cannot be lost again, and give thanks to God. It can be helpful to tell someone about your decision, preferably someone you know to be a sincere Christian.

GETTING TO KNOW GOD

As a new Christian you have entered into a brand-new relationship with God. Your new relationship needs developing and protecting. You develop any relationship with a person by spending time with them, to learn about them and get to know them. It is exactly the same with God; he wants you to spend time with him to get to know him and grow stronger as a Christian. There are three main ways in which to develop your relationship with God: finding out about him in the Bible, speaking to him in prayer, and through being with other Christians.

Reading what God says – in the Bible

God wants to speak to you. One of the main ways he does this is through the Bible. Christians believe that the Bible is God's Word, written by a large number of writers under the direct inspiration of the Holy Spirit. The Bible is therefore of vital importance to us.

In it God reveals things about himself – who he is, what he is like, what his purposes are, who Jesus is, what Jesus did during his life on earth and why he did it, the point of life, what happens when we die, what sin is and why it matters, how God has saved us, how God wants us to live, how to serve God... and so much more. In fact, through the Bible we can discover everything we need to know to succeed in the Christian life.

> All Scripture is God-breathed and is useful for teaching, rebuking, correcting and training in righteousness, so that the servant of God may be thoroughly equipped for every good work.
> 2 Timothy 3:16–17

The Bible is an exciting book full of real-life stories. God's plan has always been for the world to relate to him. Therefore,

> For everything that was written in the past was written to teach us, so that through the endurance taught in the Scriptures and the encouragement they provide we might have hope.
> Romans 15:4

the way he has chosen to speak to us is by recording his interaction with mankind in the Bible. Throughout it we read of God's initiative in reaching out to men and women and their response back to God. It is a frank and honest account of God's unfailing goodness set against all the highs and lows of people's lives as they pass into and out of obedience to him. The Bible is therefore not an indexed subject manual. Rather it is an insight into our own true nature, and God's, through a record of how he has worked in the lives of individuals, families and nations.

Christians also believe that the Bible is God's *living* Word. This means that it is not just a record of the past, but a channel through which God communicates today. God speaks to us through the Bible.

> For the word of God is alive and active. Sharper than any double-edged sword, it penetrates even to dividing soul and spirit, joints and marrow; it judges the thoughts and attitudes of the heart.
> Hebrews 4:12

Through the presence of the Holy Spirit, God's Word comes to life. God helps us to understand its meaning and shows us how to apply it to our lives.

> But the Advocate, the Holy Spirit ... will teach you all things and will remind you of everything I have said to you.
> John 14:26

As we read, God will answer our questions, guide us, instruct us, discipline us, inspire us, fill us with wonder and praise, command us, encourage us, warn us, comfort us, teach and develop us. Through the Bible we get to know God better and better, and the more we get to know him, the more we will want to know.

> Therefore everyone who hears these words of mine and puts them into practice is like a wise man who built his house on the rock.
> Matthew 7:24

To make reading the Bible enjoyable, you will need to get hold of a modern, easy-to-read version of the Bible. It is best to start reading in the New Testament, particularly the first four books (the Gospels) which cover the life of Jesus. Buying a set of daily Bible-reading notes is also a good idea; these set a daily reading for you and bring out some helpful and interesting points. The idea is to learn about God and the Christian life, and then work out how to put what you learn into practice.

Talking with God – in prayer

If the Bible is the one of the main ways in which we hear from God, then prayer is one of the main ways we can speak to God. Two-way

> And pray in the Spirit on all occasions with all kinds of prayers and requests.
> Ephesians 6:18

communication is central to any relationship, and God longs for us to talk to him. He asks us to bring everything to him in prayer, to bare our souls to him, to share all our hopes and

> Devote yourselves to prayer, being watchful and thankful.
> Colossians 4:2

desires, our fears and anxieties, our needs and our joys.

God wants us to praise and worship him, to tell him we love him, to ask him to help us, to ask him to help others and to thank him. It is also in prayer that we get ourselves cleaned up from our mistakes. As Christians we continue to

GOD'S LOVE AND TRUTH

get it wrong; when we do, we must come to him and confess everything we have thought, said or done that we know to be wrong. He is faithful to us and will forgive us.

> For the eyes of the Lord are on the righteous and his ears are attentive to their prayer.
> 1 Peter 3:12

There is no absolutely right or wrong way to pray. Nor are there any prescriptive words you must use. God just wants us to express ourselves to him in our own words, with love and trust in our hearts. You can pray anywhere, anyhow – standing up, sitting down, eyes open, eyes closed, on the move or shut away, for a few seconds or hours, silently or out loud, alone or with others – God will hear you, always.

Whatever our circumstances, God always hears our prayer. However, to make the most of your own personal and private prayers it is best to try and find a place where you can be quiet and alone. You also need enough time so that

> enter the Most Holy Place by the blood of Jesus, by a new and living way opened up for us ... let us draw near to God with a sincere heart and with the full assurance that faith brings
> Hebrews 10:19–22

you can feel relaxed and unpressured. God is the Almighty Creator, but he is also your warm loving Father; he has all the time in the world to spend with you. He holds the whole world in his hands, but you are his dear son or daughter and he wants to hear every little thing on your heart. He loves you very deeply and tenderly; every care you have becomes his care too. Come before him with respect, but also come before him with utter confidence and know his loving embrace. Pour out your heart to him; tell it all.

As you grow in confidence in prayer with God, you should

> Be still, and know that I am God
> Psalm 46:10

also learn to listen. God will speak to you in the quietness of your heart. As you wait on him, he will impress things upon you through the Holy Spirit. Perhaps he will give you a thought, or perhaps he will impress a visual image or particular word on your mind. As your relationship with God grows deeper, it will become ever more exciting.

Time with God each day

Reading the Bible and praying are two of the main ways in which Christians develop their personal relationship with God. You have spiritual needs and these can only

> Look to the LORD and his strength; seek his face always.
> 1 Chronicles 16:11

be satisfied by spending time with God regularly and often. It is as important as food and water; you need your spiritual food, or you will become weak. It is impossible to stay still in the Christian life – either you move forward or you fall back. God is the limitless source of all you need, so come into his presence and richly enjoy all he wants to give you. Try to have a 'quiet time' with God each day. Find a spot in the day that suits you and persevere with it; you will be blessed. Spend time reading the Bible and praying. In the following chapter there are some more practical suggestions on how to go about doing these things.

WHY CHURCH MATTERS

The third main way in which Christians develop their relationship with God is through being part of a church community. Everyone needs to receive love and support, encouragement and guidance, teaching and instruction. The church is the God-given family environment in which this happens. The church is actually the group of people who meet together; the physical church building is just the meeting place.

> Now you are the body of Christ, and each one of you is a part of it.
> 1 Corinthians 12:27

In becoming a Christian, God has adopted you as his child, alongside every other person who has become a Christian. This means that all Christians are related to each other; we are all members of one family. This family is called the church, not a building but the people. Jesus is the head of the church, and all other Christians are our spiritual brothers and sisters.

> you are no longer foreigners and strangers, but fellow citizens with God's people and also members of his household
> Ephesians 2:19

Christianity is therefore not about individuals, but about believers together. Anyone who tries to be an independent Christian will be weak and vulnerable. Ultimately they may not be able to bear up under the temptations and worldly pressures around them. They are likely to grow cold; they will certainly miss out enormously on all that God wants for them. Belonging to a church is a vital part of the Christian life.

> Therefore encourage one another and build each other up
> 1 Thessalonians 5:11

Church is a place to worship and praise God, be strengthened and built up, to enjoy friendships, receive teaching and learn, pray together, grow and develop. It is a place to help others as well as to be helped, to give of yourself to God and serve him. Church is also the place where you can be baptised and take part in Communion with other Christians.

Worshipping God

A real highlight of the Christian life is the opportunity to worship God. When worship is as it should be, it is a unique experience that touches us at all levels of our mind, emotions and spirit. It is at times thrilling

> I will give thanks to you, LORD, with all my heart; I will tell of all your wonderful deeds. I will be glad and rejoice in you; I will sing the praises of your name, O Most High.
> Psalm 9:1-2

and uplifting and at other times soothing and calming. The power of God's presence can flood us with a real sense of his love, joy and peace. So much so that we will want to linger in his presence as long as possible. This is especially true when we gather together with other Christians and are open to God moving amongst us. God longs for us to lovingly worship him, but he not only wants us to worship, he even commands that we do. He does not do this simply for his own pleasure, but for our pleasure and well-being.

> For great is the LORD and most worthy of praise
> Psalm 96:4

God deeply loves us and he is delighted when we express our love back to him through worship. God is worthy of our highest possible praise. He is our great and glorious God who has reached out to us and saved us, even though we did not deserve it. He offers us his unfailing help and has promised us eternal happiness in heaven.

There is so much to thank and praise God for, but we need to learn to allow the Holy Spirit to release the ability

GOD'S LOVE AND TRUTH

> God is spirit, and his worshippers must worship in the Spirit and in truth.
> John 4:24

to worship from within us. As we spend time with God we begin to discover just how inspiring his presence is. In God's presence, passion and desire for him begin to well up inside us; we will want to worship him. Our in-built desire for God is awakened and released by the Holy Spirit who lives in us.

Our worship certainly pleases God, but it also meets some of our own most basic needs as well. It is an essential activity for our spiritual health and overall well-being. When we worship God we become more focused on him and less focused on ourselves. This helps us with the process of becoming more God-centred. We start to become people of faith who depend on God rather than self-centred people who are proud and independent.

> Praise the LORD. Sing to the LORD a new song ... Let them praise his name with dancing and make music to him with tambourine and harp. For the LORD takes delight in his people
> Psalm 149:1–4

> So then, just as you received Christ Jesus as Lord, continue to live your lives in him, rooted and built up in him, strengthened in the faith as you were taught, and overflowing with thankfulness.
> Colossians 2:6–7

As we worship God, we become strengthened and changed by being in his presence. Our minds are reminded of his greatness, of all that he has done, of our security in him, of his promises to us and of the eternal future he has planned for us in heaven. Our emotions are soothed and comforted by his peace; they are excited by his power and glory; we feel accepted, valued, loved and cared for. Our spirits are fed and nourished, strengthened and empowered. Without worship we will quickly become cool towards God, grow weak and falter. Worship renews our desire for God, restores the right perspectives, helps us grow stronger, and moves us forward.

> speaking to one another with psalms, hymns, and songs from the Spirit. Sing and make music in your heart to the Lord, always giving thanks to God the Father for everything, in the name of our Lord Jesus Christ.
> *Ephesians 5:19–20*

There are many ways in which we can worship God. We can thank and praise him in prayer, we can recite words of praise from the Bible, or sing worship songs. Some people use dance, drama, painting, music and many other means of expressing themselves. In fact we can worship God through any activity that focuses on God and glorifies him. All these things can be done alone and indeed God wants us to worship him privately. However, this is no replacement for worshipping him alongside other Christians. There is great blessing in worshipping with others. Nothing can replace the power of God's presence in a large gathering of sincere Christians all seeking to glorify God together.

Baptism

Baptism is an exciting and very important event in a Christian's life. It is something that is done once only. The person concerned is immersed in water (or has water poured over them) as they are baptised in the name of the Father and of the Son and of the

> We were therefore buried with him through baptism into death in order that, just as Christ was raised from the dead through the glory of the Father, we too may live a new life.
> *Romans 6:4*

Holy Spirit. The act of baptism identifies the Christian with the death, burial and resurrection of Christ, and symbolises the spiritual washing away of the dirt of sin. It is often also associated with coming into full fellowship in the church.

> Therefore go and make disciples of all nations, baptising them in the name of the Father and of the Son and of the Holy Spirit
> Matthew 28:19

Every Christian should be baptised. It is so important that Jesus commanded every believer to do so. When you are baptised you are making a public profession of your faith in Jesus. You are saying to all that you have died to your old sinful way of life and risen up to a new spiritual life instead. You are declaring your allegiance to Christ and unity with the family of believers. Through your actions you are also being a witness to others, showing them the way to be saved.

Baptism is a confirmation of your agreement with God to live his way. It is an occasion to expect to experience the joy that comes by being obedient to God and to receive the blessing of Jesus as he anoints you through the power of the Holy Spirit.

Communion

Another special activity that takes place in church is Holy Communion (also called the Eucharist, the Lord's Supper or the breaking of bread). Communion, which is held regularly, involves eating a small piece of 'bread' and taking a sip of 'wine'. The bread is used to represent Christ's body, which he gave for us on the cross. The wine represents the blood he shed. During Communion we remember what Jesus has done for us and give him thanks. He died for us,

> he took bread, gave thanks and broke it, and gave it to them, saying, 'This is my body given for you; do this in remembrance of me.' In the same way, after the supper he took the cup, saying, 'This cup is the new covenant in my blood, which is poured out for you.'
> Luke 22:19–20

was raised to life and is coming back. We have been forgiven for every wrong and we have eternal life. There is so much for us to joyfully praise him for.

Before taking part in Communion it is important to make sure we are right with God and right with other people. We need to confess any unforgiven wrongdoing. We also need to forgive others who have hurt us and try to make amends where a relationship has become clouded. It is also a time to recommit ourselves to God, to renew our resolve to live in obedience to him; to love him and to love each other.

> the Spirit of him who raised Jesus from the dead is living in you
> Romans 8:11

Sharing Communion with our fellow Christians in the church helps us maintain a close relationship with God and with each other. It is an activity that we do together as a family. When we participate with faith and the right attitude, we will be blessed by God. Jesus himself will spiritually nourish and strengthen us by working in us through the Holy Spirit.

See chapter 6 for some practical suggestions to help you get going in reading the Bible and praying, and to help you find the right church to go to.

PUTTING FAITH INTO ACTION – LIVING THE CHRISTIAN LIFE

Christian faith involves believing that what God says is absolutely true. However, it goes further than this. It also involves putting our faith

> Do not merely listen to the word, and so deceive yourselves. Do what it says.
> James 1:22

into practice; we need to act on our beliefs. If our faith is genuine then it should lead to different behaviour in our lives, behaviour that pleases God rather than just ourselves. If there is no evidence of changes beginning to take place in our behaviour, it is a sign that we have not really taken the step of trusting God.

> His divine power has given us everything we need for a godly life
> 2 Peter 1:3

God may ask us to do things we feel we cannot do, and to change in ways we think we cannot change. Our immediate response might be to say, 'I can't do it!' When we respond this way we are actually partly right; we could not do it if it were simply up to us. However, faith means trusting God to enable us to do things that seem beyond us. God provides us with the power and the strength. We in turn must supply the willingness and the obedience. We need to say 'yes' to God, then do what he asks in faith that he will keep his promises to us and enable us to do it. We can't do it alone. Nor will God do it all for us. He wants us to work with him; this is part of the relationship.

One of the key things God asks us to do in faith is to overcome sin in our lives. Our relationship with God needs both developing and protecting. We develop our relationship with God by spending time with him. We protect our

> You were taught, with regard to your former way of life, to put off your old self, which is being corrupted by its deceitful desires; to be made new in the attitude of your minds; and to put on the new self, created to be like God in true righteousness and holiness.
> *Ephesians 4:22–24*

relationship with him by avoiding anything that damages it. Sin comes between us and God. It profoundly affects what we are, how we think and how we feel. When we fall short we sadden God, we hurt ourselves and we hurt other people around us as well.

Unfortunately we don't seem to get very far before we mess up; we make mistakes. However, our relationship with God has to be maintained, so God commands us to deal with our failures. The way we do this is by *repenting*. Repentance comes in two parts. The first part involves coming to God to get cleaned up, by asking him

> If we confess our sins, he is faithful and just and will forgive us our sins and purify us from all unrighteousness.
> *1 John 1:9*

to forgive us. We need to come to him humbly and sincerely, and tell him we are sorry for whatever has put us in the wrong. Doing this involves the difficult task of overcoming our natural pride, objections and excuses. But if we ask him for his forgiveness we can be assured that he will always give it to us; this is his promise. When we have asked, we should not doubt but believe that we are permanently forgiven. We only need to confess one time. Once it is done, it is over and done with, forever; the sin is obliterated and we are clean again.

> But thanks be to God! He gives us the victory through our Lord Jesus Christ.
> *1 Corinthians 15:57*

If the first part of repentance can sometimes be hard, the

second part can often be harder. We must set out to change and put the problem behaviour behind us. To do this we need to rely on God's strength. He will provide the power we need, but we must provide the willingness and the determination to obey him. There is a battle going on. The battle of our new godly nature against our old defiant nature. We have the power to overcome. We have the fullness of Jesus Christ in us. Christ is Lord over all, he is the victor over sin and we have nothing to fear. If we fail again, then we simply come to God and ask his forgiveness again. We never give up. Thanks to God's infinite love and mercy there is no limit to his forgiveness for the Christian who sincerely asks for it. We have permission to keep coming back, again and again.

> Follow God's example, therefore, as dearly loved children and live a life of love
> Ephesians 5:1–2

God asks us to live in obedience to him. Turning away from all that is wrong is part of it, but there is more. He wants us to be like him! God's desire is for us to grow and develop in such a way that we start to display his character. God is not satisfied with just getting rid of what is bad in us; he wants to fill us with his goodness. We are to stop doing wrong and start being a blessing instead.

God is love and like him we are to love. This is God's greatest command to us – to love God above all else and then to love others as ourselves. The more time we spend with God, the more he changes us and starts to form his character in us. We

> 'Love the Lord your God with all your heart and with all your soul and with all your mind.' This is the first and greatest commandment. And the second is like it: 'Love your neighbour as yourself.'
> Matthew 22:37–39

must learn to allow the inner changes to work their way out. We are to live differently in obedience to God, by being good and doing good. We are to have different attitudes and different priorities. We are not to conform to the world's compromising standards and selfish attitudes; we are to conform to God's holy standards and selfless attitudes. In this way we will glorify God with our lives.

> make every effort to add to your faith goodness; and to goodness, knowledge; and to knowledge, self-control; and to self-control, perseverance; and to perseverance, godliness; and to godliness, and to godliness, mutual affection; and to mutual affection, love.
> 2 Peter 1:5–7

Our role model is Jesus himself. He is the one we are to be like. Jesus never fell short in any way; he always lived in complete obedience to God his Father. He is the only person of perfectly good character who has ever lived. Jesus devoted himself to doing good, unselfishly giving his all for the benefit of others. He taught people the truth about God and showed them how they could be saved. He demonstrated the love of God by his acts of compassion and kindness, and he demonstrated the power of God by his miracles. Similarly we are to obey our Father in heaven, to serve him and others by doing good, to bless others through the power of God, and to share the good news of the Christian message.

GOD'S COMMANDS AND INSTRUCTIONS FOR CHRISTIAN LIVING

God asks us to obey him, but what does this actually mean? How does he want us to live? We discover the answer to this

> Direct me in the path of your commands, for there I find delight.
> Psalm 119:35

by studying the Bible and by learning from the teaching and example of godly people at church. Some of the key areas we need to address in our lives have already been touched on above. To help a little more, here is a summary of some of the main ways in which we are to obey God.

Love God
- Give God first place in our lives, make him our priority; love, respect and obey him
- Spend time with God, develop our personal relationship with him
- Study the Bible to discover for ourselves what God is really like, let him reveal himself to us
- Worship him in praise and prayer, with joy and thanksgiving

Love others
- Let the love God gives us show through our love for all other people
- Consider the needs of others as much as our own needs, do good to others
- Develop a selfless character marked by such things as: patience, kindness, goodness, gentleness, self-control, honesty, generosity, humility and forgiveness
- Show a special care for other Christians: those in the family of believers

Grow in knowledge, faith and obedience
- Live a life based on faith in God; trust him, believe in him and depend on him
- Study the Bible to learn how God wants us to live

- Do what God says, put what we learn into practice, be obedient to him
- Desire to grow into maturity as a Christian, seek after God and let him change us

Serve God
- Offer ourselves to God, allow him to use us to do his work, be a blessing to people inside and outside the church
- Share the faith we have, be a witness by the way we live, tell others about Jesus
- Pray for others, intercede for them, bring God's blessing and protection on them
- Give to God out of our own resources – money, time, talents and energy

Overcome sin
- Turn away from the things we know to be wrong, resist temptation and do not give up
- Fight against our old character that is spoiled by such things as: pride, arrogance, jealousy, selfishness, resentment, anger, retaliation, lust, greed, sexual impurity, dishonesty, gossip, drunkenness and bad language
- Confess our failures to God, receive his forgiveness and renew our determination to resist temptation
- Forgive others just as God forgives us, show mercy to others just as God has shown mercy to us

Growing and developing in these ways is our life's work. It is a journey during which we grow and change. Becoming a Christian is just the start.

Appendices 1 and 2 provide some relevant verses from the Bible that encourage us in our walk with God and help us understand what he asks of us.

WHAT TO EXPECT – THE REALITY

In becoming a Christian you have entered into the place of God's blessing. You now enjoy a special relationship with him and come under his powerful and loving care and protection. You have been saved from your old way of life and set free to live a new and better way instead.

> I will say of the LORD, 'He is my refuge and my fortress, my God, in whom I trust.'
> Psalm 91:2

> In this world you will have trouble. But take heart! I have overcome the world.
> John 16:33

With all of these wonderful changes it can be easy to form wrong expectations of the Christian life. For example, you might be tempted to believe that your life should suddenly be completely sorted out and that everything should fall neatly into place. You may start expecting all of life's struggles and problems to become a thing of the past and believe that every day should now pass with sublime smoothness and happiness. Unfortunately this is not a right understanding of the Christian life. It is not always going to be easy and it is not going to be trouble free. It should be rich, it should be fulfilling, it is the right way to live and it will lead to eternal happiness. But it will also be challenging and sometimes costly. Be warned, the Christian life is not a soft option!

Why do Christians face trials and difficulties?

> Those who live according to the flesh have their minds set on what the flesh desires; but those who live in accordance with the Spirit have their minds set on what the Spirit desires.
> *Romans 8:5*

The world we live in is not perfect and none of the people in it are perfect either. This is why we needed to be saved. Our salvation changes our eternal destiny. It also changes the way we are able to live. It does not, however, mean that we have become perfect; we haven't, we are still fallible. Christians are imperfect people living in an imperfect world. We are therefore bound to share in the suffering that afflicts everyone.

> Dear friends, do not be surprised at the fiery ordeal that has come on you to test you, as though something strange were happening to you. But rejoice inasmuch as you participate in the sufferings of Christ, so that you may be overjoyed when his glory is revealed.
> *1 Peter 4:12–13*

At the beginning of time God's creation was perfect, but the world turned away from God and became spoiled. At the end of time God will restore perfection once again. Then we will be made perfect and there will be a new perfect heaven and new perfect earth. However, in-between these two points in history lies the mess of sin. It is in this fallen world that Christians must continue to live until we die or Jesus returns. So the Christian life is not going to be all rosy. It is the best option but it is not the easiest option!

Some of the challenges you will face as a Christian

One of the biggest challenges we face as Christians is simply the task of enduring life's trials in a way that pleases God. We are fallible people living in a spoiled world. Each

> Consider it pure joy, my brothers and sisters, whenever you face trials of many kinds, because you know that the testing of your faith produces perseverance. Let perseverance finish its work so that you may be mature and complete, not lacking anything.
> James 1:2–4

of us will be touched by the suffering that plagues everyone. Mostly it will be in the form of everyday frustrations and disappointments. However, we may also suffer in more serious ways that deeply test our faith.

God has not promised to make us immune from problems and difficulties. He has, however, promised to take us through the difficult times if we will trust him. To those who love God, he has promised to turn every bad experience into something good. God's

> And we know that in all things God works for the good of those who love him.
> Romans 8:28

plan is to bring eternal benefit out of our suffering. If we respond with the right attitude and with faith, God will turn our suffering to our advantage. He will shape and mould us, refine and purify us. Through our obedient faith we will store up for ourselves things of eternal value.

> Then Jesus said to his disciples, 'Whoever wants to be my disciple must deny themselves and take up their cross and follow me.'
> Matthew 16:24

Making sacrifices is another challenge of the Christian life. This may involve giving up things we do not really want to give up. It may also mean doing things we do not always feel like doing. There may be things in our lives that we know are really not right, or that simply get in the way of our relationship with God, but we do not want to let go of them. We may be reluctant to devote enough time to building our relationship with God and serving him. We may also be reticent to be kind to people who hurt us or irritate us.

God will convict us of the things in our lives he wants to change. Our inner response might well be, 'But I don't want to!' The reason we tend to object like this is because of the inner battle that goes on between our old character and the new one God is forming in us. However, we must work at overcoming such feelings and desires if we are to obey God and grow. We are to decide to agree with the new nature God has given us and reject the old one that tries to cling on.

> but we also glory in our sufferings, because we know that suffering produces perseverance; perseverance, character; and character, hope. And hope does not put us to shame, because God's love has been poured out into our hearts through the Holy Spirit, who has been given to us.
> *Romans 5:3–5*

> If the world hates you, keep in mind that it hated me first. If you belonged to the world, it would love you as its own. As it is, you do not belong to the world, but I have chosen you out of the world. That is why the world hates you.
> *John 15:18–19*

Withstanding opposition is a further challenge we may face. The world does not know God but has rejected him. By entering into a relationship with Jesus, we have become filled with his presence. We may not realise it, but in an unseen way we give off something of the light of Christ within us. Therefore, we too can at times expect rejection from the world. To help us, we must remember that our true identity comes from Christ; it is what he thinks that really matters. Jesus asks us to respond with grace and in love. The way to win is to overcome evil with good.

> Be alert and of sober mind. Your enemy the devil prowls around like a roaring lion looking for someone to devour. Resist him, standing firm in the faith
> 1 Peter 5:8–9

Ungodly people are not the only wrong influences in our lives. God warns us that there are also unseen evil spiritual powers at work. The Bible highlights the existence of an evil spiritual being called Satan (the devil). Satan was once a glorious angel in heaven, but he became proud and envious of God and grasped at power and glory for himself. He wanted to be worshipped rather than to worship his Creator. Evil entered him and he was expelled from God's presence in heaven, together with all those who followed him. Now Satan is God's enemy; he utterly hates God and lives in incessant opposition to everything God loves. What God loves most is his people. Therefore, Satan is out to ruin our relationship with God. He tempts us and distracts us, he lies to us and tries to delude us, he aims to discourage us and drag us down. Jesus has already defeated Satan through what he accomplished on the cross. God has appointed the time for him to face final judgement, and the outcome is certain. Until then, Satan can influence us, but he has no control over us; we belong to the Kingdom of God. Therefore, if we resist him, he will retreat and flee from us.

How do Christians get through the tough times?

We should not be surprised when we experience frustrations, struggles, doubts and disappointment, or when

> For I am convinced that neither death nor life, neither angels nor demons, neither the present nor the future, nor any powers, neither height nor depth, nor anything else in all creation, will be able to separate us from the love of God that is in Christ Jesus our Lord.
> Romans 8:38–39

people set themselves against us because of our faith. We need to be prepared to face difficulty. The way we do this is by taking God's hand and walking through life with him. This means that we are to depend on him, trust him and believe in his promises. He will lead us and guide us, help and strengthen us, and give his comfort and peace.

Our example is Jesus himself. He was not spared suffering but went through the greatest of trials, without yielding to temptation and without complaining or sliding into self-pity. Jesus fully trusted God, knowing that God loved him. We should do the same. Nothing can separate us from the love of God. We are to be motivated by thankfulness and by the prospect of heaven. When we think about Jesus we should be thankful to him for saving us, and want to trust him and be like him. When we consider heaven, we should be uplifted at the thought of all the joy that is in store for us and be encouraged to persevere.

> And let us run with perseverance the race marked out for us, fixing our eyes on Jesus, the pioneer and perfecter of faith. For the joy that was set before him he endured the cros
> Hebrews 12:1–2

To be strong and endure the testing times, we must always hold on firmly to God's truths; we cannot rely on our feelings. Our feelings are unreliable and variable. God's truth is completely reliable and unchanging. Sometimes we may feel that God is very far away. The truth is that he is actually very close. At other times we may feel helpless and without direction. The truth is that God is in control. How we stand with God is not a matter of our

> Let us hold unswervingly to the hope we profess, for he who promised is faithful.
> Hebrews 10:23

GOD'S LOVE AND TRUTH

feelings but a matter of truth. What God says is how things really are, despite what our senses may be telling us. We need to learn to believe this, whatever our circumstances.

This does not mean that feelings do not matter to God; they do. God knows exactly how we feel and cares deeply about our emotional well-being. He shares in our struggles and, if we let him, he brings us through them. But we must learn to rely on the truth. By living in faith first, positive feelings have fertile ground in which to grow. God calls this building on the solid rock of his truth, instead of on the shifting sands of our feelings and emotions.

> I have learned the secret of being content in any and every situation ... I can do all this through him who gives me strength.
> Philippians 4:12–13

> Therefore, as we have opportunity, let us do good to all people, especially to those who belong to the family of believers.
> Galatians 6:10

Maintaining a strong personal relationship with God is vital if we are to get through the tough times. But there is more help at hand. As Christians we have become part of a very large family. This is what the church is. We have become spiritual brothers and sisters, and like all good families God's intention is that we love and support each other. Therefore, we need to turn to other Christians and allow them to come alongside us, to pray for us and pray with us, to offer encouragement and wise advice, and to provide practical help and support in whatever way they can. Similarly we should do the same for them, as we are able and when we have the opportunity.

GOD'S PROMISES AND WORDS OF ENCOURAGEMENT

> Because of the LORD's great love we are not consumed, for his compassions never fail. They are new every morning; great is your faithfulness.
> *Lamentations 3:22–23*

To have a healthy relationship with God it is vital that we are led by his truth and not by the vagaries of our hearts. To help us, God's Word is filled with his promises to Christians. Here is a summary of some of the main ones. Included within Appendix 1 are some of the many helpful verses in the Bible that can help us in each of these areas.

You are saved
- God gladly receives *everyone* who comes to him in faith
- Your every failing has been forgiven forever, you belong to Jesus Christ and you cannot be lost
- You have been set free from guilt and saved from the penalty of sin
- You can face God with utter confidence because you have been made righteous and holy by Christ

You have eternal life
- Jesus has prepared a place for you in heaven
- Jesus will return, and one day you will live with him in perfect happiness forever
- You have been adopted into God's family and become one of his special children
- You will be rewarded for your faith and for the good you have done, and will share in Christ's inheritance

God's favour and presence rest on you
- God's love for you is wholehearted, unconditional and everlasting
- God will be completely faithful to you, he can always be totally trusted
- You have the presence of God with you through his Spirit, he will never leave you
- God is your refuge, he offers you his comfort and peace in times of trouble

God watches over you
- God is your all-powerful Father, he holds you completely safe in his loving arms
- He watches over you, he will strengthen and protect you, as you live in his will
- He knows all your needs before you ask, he will provide and care for you as you trust and obey him
- He has a plan for you, he will guide your steps and lead you through your life

God will empower you
- You have been given the Holy Spirit; Jesus lives in you, he will give you his power and strength
- The Holy Spirit will enable you to hear God speaking to your heart, he will reveal God's will to you, he will help you to understand the Bible, and he will lead you in prayer and worship
- The Holy Spirit will give you the power to break free from bad habits, the power to resist temptation, and the ability to become more like Jesus
- The Holy Spirit will equip you with gifts, enabling you to be powerful and effective in your service for God

6

Some Practical Help

> The first thing Andrew did was to find his brother Simon and tell him, 'We have found the Messiah' (that is, the Christ). And he brought him to Jesus.
> John 1:41

Reading the Bible, praying and being part of a church are some of the key activities that form part of the Christian life. If you have no background in Christianity, or even if you do, you may be asking, 'Where do I start?' *How* do I read my Bible and pray? *How* do I find a good church? Perhaps you already know someone who is a sincere Christian; perhaps there is a friend, colleague or relative you could turn to for some help. If you approach them and tell them you have become a Christian and are looking for some guidance, they should be very pleased to help you. However, if there is no-one, or you do not want to approach them, what then?

HOW DO YOU FIND THE RIGHT CHURCH TO GO TO?

> Christ is the head of the church, his body, of which he is the Saviour.
> *Ephesians 5:23*

Perhaps the first question should be, 'What makes a good church?' Every Christian you ask is likely to give a slightly different answer to this question, because they have slightly different views or preferences. However, there are certain key values that make a church 'good' in God's eyes. A good church is one where:

- Jesus is at the centre of everything; he is the focus of attention
- The beliefs of the leadership and the teaching from the front are firmly based on the Bible
- There is a healthy balance of worship, prayer, teaching and outreach
- There is an atmosphere of love and unity
- The people are welcoming and friendly to everyone who comes in
- There is a sense of vibrancy with a variety of activities going on through the week
- There is a real concern for the world outside and not just for themselves

> Finally, all of you, be like-minded, be sympathetic, love one another, be compassionate and humble.
> *1 Peter 3:8*

No church is perfect. However, some churches are spiritually stronger than others and are more committed to moving forward. God's greatest blessings fall on those churches he finds to be filled with love and truth, and where the Holy Spirit is given freedom to do his work.

SOME PRACTICAL HELP

> For where two or three gather in my name, there am I with them.
> *Matthew 18:20*

There is a great variety of styles to be found in different churches; from the traditional and fairly formal, to the relaxed and informal, right through to the alternative types of church aimed at the younger generations or based directly within the community. Churches also vary greatly in size; from those where thousands meet in large purpose-built premises, to those consisting of only a handful of people who get together in someone's home. Bigger churches obviously have better resources, but it is not really size that matters. Rather it is the spiritual qualities of the church and the direction it is moving in.

> To the angel of the church in Ephesus ... I know your deeds, your hard work and your perseverance ... Yet I hold this against you: you have forsaken the love you had at first.
> *Revelation 2:1–4*

Any of the major national Christian church groups (denominations) are 'sound' in terms of what they teach, but there can be a tremendous variety in the spiritual depth and vibrancy of life that is to be found in them. If you are fortunate enough to be presented with a choice of good churches then it is very much a matter of finding the place that seems right for you. However, always make absolutely sure that the teaching is firmly based on a widely accepted version of the Christian Bible (i.e. it is an *evangelical* church) – ask the question. There are many different evangelical churches; the mainstream ones are Anglican, Methodist and Baptist, but there are many others, including independent evangelical churches and networks.

So how do you find and choose the right church to join?

> I will instruct you and teach you in the way you should go; I will counsel you with my loving eye on you.
> Psalm 32:8

- Pray about it; ask God to help you
- Find out what churches there are within reach
- Ask people you know
- Look on the internet for church websites
- Enquire at a local Christian bookshop (if there is one)
- Look under 'Places of Worship' in a business telephone directory
- Look at adverts in local newspapers
- Refer to the list of churches running the Alpha course (see later)
- Visit some of them
- Find out when they meet
- Go often enough to give them a chance; try different meetings at different times, both on a Sunday and during the week
- Talk to the people who go regularly and to the leaders; ask them questions
- Make a decision
- Keep praying
- Choose the place that seems right (do you feel at peace about your decision?)
- Make a commitment to stay and get yourself involved quickly
- What activities are there for new Christians or new members – small groups to join or a course to sign up for?

The Alpha Course

One Christian course that is worth a special mention is 'Alpha'. Alpha is a Christian basics course that covers some of life's important questions. Alpha courses are now running all around the world. They are aimed at anyone wanting to investigate Christianity, as well as new Christians and those who want to brush up on the basics.

> I hear about ... your faith in the Lord Jesus ... Your love has given me great joy and encouragement
>
> Philemon 5–7

Alpha is fun to do; the atmosphere is relaxed and friendly, and often humorous. The organisers work hard to make the environment welcoming and supportive to everyone, whoever they are, whatever their beliefs and background. Anyone who comes can be confident that they will be accepted and not be pressurised in any way. Any question goes and any point of view can be expressed. Each of the weekly sessions usually starts with a social time, and a meal may be served. There is then a short and interesting talk followed by relaxed discussion in small groups. Over a period of about ten weeks a number of questions are answered about the Christian faith. Alpha looks at who Jesus is, why he died, being sure of your faith, praying, reading the Bible, receiving God's guidance, what the Holy Spirit does, resisting evil, telling others about Jesus, healing, the church, and making the most of your life.

Information on Alpha can be found on their website, www.alpha.org, which also contains a register of churches running Alpha all over the world.

READING THE BIBLE – GETTING STARTED

> I love those who love me, and those who seek me find me.
> *Proverbs 8:17*

Bible reading forms an essential part of our personal quiet times with God. Our quiet times are the times we regularly spend alone with God, ideally every day, reading his Word and praying. These quiet times are vital to our spiritual health and development.

In the past you would probably have had only one choice of Bible, The Authorised Version (also called the King James Version). Although it is extremely well regarded, it was written in the old style of English used in the 1600s. Many people would now find it difficult to read and understand. Fortunately we are now spoiled for choice; there are numerous modern translations that are easy and interesting to read.

> Jesus answered, 'It is written: "Man shall not live on bread alone, but on every word that comes from the mouth of God."'
> *Matthew 4:4*

Modern translations are available in a wide range of different formats. Apart from straightforward Bibles, which contain only the Bible text, there are many versions that come with all sorts of additional information. These Bibles contain such things as explanatory notes to aid understanding, cross-references, maps, pictures, various indexes, and even practical guidance on how to apply what is being said to our lives. There are also special versions for children and teenagers. Most of these Bibles are available as downloadable applications for mobile devices or within more advanced packages for computers.

Choose a version that appeals to you; it is important

that you feel comfortable with it and will enjoy reading it. Check which translation is most widely used in the church you go to. It may be useful to have the same one, although it is not essential. Two very popular translations, favoured for their precise faithfulness to the original Bible texts, are the New International Version (NIV) and the New King James Version (NKJV). Even easier-to-read versions, using simplified language or paraphrasing, include the New Living Translation (NLT) and *The Message*. There are many more.

What is in the Bible?

The Bible is actually a collection of books, sixty-six in all. It is more like a library of books rather than just one book. This means that it is not really a book that you open at page one and proceed to read it all the way through. At some stage you may choose to do just that, but it is not a good beginning.

The Bible is divided into two main sections, the Old Testament and the New Testament. The thirty-nine books of the Old Testament cover the period from God's creation up until the time before Jesus. The twenty-seven books of the New Testament cover the period from the coming of Jesus until the end of time, and into eternity. Within the Testaments there are various different types of book. Their content spans such things as: the creation of the world, stories about God's people (history), God's rules on how his people were to live (law), wisdom, songs and poetry (Psalms and Proverbs), God's messages to his people about

> How sweet are your words to my taste, sweeter than honey to my mouth! I gain understanding from your precepts; therefore I hate every wrong path. Your word is a lamp for my feet, a light on my path.
> Psalm 119:103–105

their present circumstances and future (prophecy), the life of Jesus (the Gospels) and letters to the early church. Some detail on how the books of the Bible fit together is included in Appendix 3.

Each book of the Bible is divided into chapters, and each chapter is divided into verses. This is done simply to enable any passage to be readily identified and found again. The divisions are the same for every translation. For example, a 'reference' might be: 'the book of John, chapter 3 and verses 16 to 17'. Usually this is abbreviated to something like, 'Jn 3:16–17'. At the front of every Bible there is an index of the contents, giving the page numbers for every book.

How do you go about reading the Bible?

It is a good idea to buy some daily Bible notes from a Christian bookseller. There are many different ones to try, including some specifically written for new Christians. Daily notes set you a short Bible passage to read, and give you some helpful comments or illustrations to bring out the important points. Using notes takes away the problem of deciding what to read and can make it easier to understand the Bible. They can also help you get into the healthy habit of reading your Bible every day.

> Keep this Book of the Law always on your lips; meditate on it day and night, so that you may be careful to do everything written in it.
> Joshua 1:8

Using notes can, however, sometimes make life a little too easy and laziness creeps in. If you want reading the Bible to be interesting and rewarding then you must be prepared to put in a little effort. If you take time to think and pray about what you read, you will get much more out of it. For this reason, some people prefer to have the freedom of choosing their own passages to read. They will tend to spend a lot more time trying to understand the Bible and work out how to apply it to their lives. To assist them, they may enlist the help of Bible commentaries that give lots of detailed notes and explanations together with some background information.

As you mature in the Christian life, this type of approach to Bible reading (or study) becomes necessary. Bible notes alone will not provide you with enough stimulation to enable you to keep growing. As you gradually learn to explore God's Word more deeply, you will discover just how rewarding it can be.

It may be helpful to adopt a fairly systematic approach to at least some of your Bible reading. This can help you get the most out of the time you spend:

- Set aside a regular daily quiet time at a point in the day that suits you
- Pray; ask God to speak to you through what you read
- Approach the time with expectancy, willing to hear and open to learn
- Read the passage through, perhaps several times, and think about it
- What does it say? Make sure you have read the passage carefully enough to know what it actually contains (and what it doesn't)
- What does it mean? What is there to be learned about God or the Christian life or the world? Is there a promise to hold on to or a command to be obeyed? (Be careful not to take short passages, single verses or sentences out of context with the overall points being made in the chapter

and book as a whole. Refer to commentaries or Bible notes to help you)
- How can it be applied? How do the things you have learned apply to you personally? How can you put them into practice? God wants us to learn and then do!
- Make notes for future reference and to remind yourself what you have learned

> Now that you know these things, you will be blessed if you do them.
> John 13:17

There are many different ways to read the Bible. The approach that is best depends on what suits you and on what your needs are. You don't always need to go through the sort of process outlined above. Sometimes you may read through a lot very quickly. At other times you may focus on just a few verses. Your desire may be to learn, or simply to know God's presence more strongly, or to find encouragement or assurance or guidance. The Bible is an amazing treasure which takes a lifetime to discover. Do not be daunted by it; instead set out to enjoy the process of discovery, in your own way and at your own pace, trusting the Holy Spirit to be your teacher and guide.

Where should I start reading?

You can buy detailed reading plans to guide you through all or part of the Bible, and these can be very helpful. In the absence of one of these, or daily notes, here are some ideas. You could start by reading:

> But when he, the Spirit of truth, comes, he will guide you into all the truth.
> John 16:13

SOME PRACTICAL HELP

1. One or all of the first three books of the New Testament (Matthew, Mark, Luke)
2. The book of John
3. The book of Acts
4. The first books of the Old Testament (Genesis and Exodus, perhaps also Deuteronomy)
5. Some or all of Paul's letters (such as Philippians and Colossians)
6. Some of the Psalms

GETTING ON WITH PRAYER

Prayer is simply talking to God. You pray to God by expressing yourself to him in words, either silently or out loud. We cannot pray too much; we can certainly pray far too little. God longs for us to talk to him and we must if we are to build our relationship with him and grow in faith. If we don't pray, we will lack spiritual strength and miss out enormously on the blessing he wants to give us. God wants to bless us. He wants to do this for our own benefit and also for the benefit of all those he wishes to bless through us.

> You, God, are my God, earnestly I seek you; I thirst for you, my whole being longs for you, in a dry and parched land where there is no water.
> Psalm 63:1

> I urge, then, first of all, that petitions, prayers, intercession and thanksgiving be made for all people
> 1 Timothy 2:1

Through prayer we are able to talk to God about all kinds of things. We can praise and thank him for all he has done. We can ask him to forgive us for our lapses in behaviour since we last confessed to him. We can pray for others who need his help, both Christians and those who are not. We can also pray for ourselves, requesting his help and strength in every situation.

> Do not be anxious about anything, but in every situation, by prayer and petition, with thanksgiving, present your requests to God.
> Philippians 4:6

God wants us to bring our every need and desire to him. He wants us to be completely honest with him and share our deepest feelings and most intimate thoughts. We can come to God with complete confidence because he deeply loves us. He has all the time in the world to listen and he is intensely interested in every tiny detail of our lives.

Prayer can seem to be all about us talking to God, but this is not actually true. Prayer also involves listening to God. This is perhaps more difficult to begin with, but necessary if our relationship is not to be all one-way. The problem is

> The LORD came and stood there, calling as at other times, 'Samuel! Samuel!' Then Samuel said, 'Speak, LORD, for your servant is listening.'
> 1 Samuel 3:10

we can be so busy telling God things that we don't bother to listen to his answers! Listening to God involves being quiet and still in his presence, whilst remaining in the attitude of prayer, and giving him a chance to impress things on our hearts and minds. This needs some practice and we need to be careful to discern what we believe is from God and what isn't.

Prayer can be engaged in anyplace, anytime, anyhow. Pray on the bus or the train, in the car or as you walk. Pray in the moment of crisis or when relaxed. Pray just a few words or pray for hours. Pray with others or alone. Pray standing, sitting, kneeling or lying down. Pray with your eyes open or shut. Pray silently or out loud.

SOME PRACTICAL HELP

> They devoted themselves to the apostles' teaching and to fellowship, to the breaking of bread and to prayer. Everyone was filled with awe at the many wonders and signs performed by the apostles
>
> Acts 2:42–43

Praying with other people can be very powerful. Tremendous answers are often received to this type of prayer. It is also an important way in which to build each other up and encourage one another. Prayer ought to be a central part of life in the church and of any small church group. It is a very good idea to find one or two others to pray with regularly, people you know well and trust so you can really share things with them.

Praying with others is very important, but praying on your own is vital. Alongside Bible reading, prayer forms an essential part of our personal quiet times with God. Through them, we develop our relationship with him and grow in love and faith.

> Very early in the morning, while it was still dark, Jesus got up, left the house and went off to a solitary place, where he prayed.
>
> Mark 1:35

How do you pray on your own?
- Try to find a time and place where you can be quietly alone with God each day, a place where you can be relaxed and unpressured, at a time when you are not too tired
- Come with an attitude of complete confidence; God is your loving Father, Jesus is your closest friend – he *always* welcomes you
- Be completely relaxed and informal, but also hold an attitude of reverence and respect. God is your loving

Father, Jesus is your friend, but he is also the Almighty Creator, the glorious and holy God who rules over all
- Physical posture does not really matter, but the inner posture of your heart does. Choose a physical posture that feels right for you, one which helps you focus on God and assists you in having the right attitude
- Try praying out loud as well as silently; this can help to make your prayers more alive and more focused
- Pray about everything and anything, perhaps make use of the following 'P-R-A-Y' reminder:

Praise and thank him; worship God for who he is, what he is like, what he has done, what he is doing, and what is to come

Repent; confess the wrong things you have done since you last prayed, forgive others who have wronged you

Another; pray for others, bring their specific needs before God, ask him to bless and protect them, pray for Christians and those who are not, pray for others to be saved

Yourself; share your heart with God, open yourself to him, be honest. Tell him your every need, desire and trouble. Ask for his help and strength. Ask him to change you and equip you to live the Christian life.

- Spend time listening to God, be quiet in his presence; give him the time and opportunity to impress himself on your thoughts, feelings and imagination
- Consider keeping a prayer notebook; list things to pray about, things to thank God for, people to pray for, your own requests and the answers God gives

SOME PRACTICAL HELP

> Our Father in heaven, hallowed be your name, your kingdom come, your will be done, on earth as in heaven. Give us today our daily bread. Forgive us our sins as we forgive those who sin against us. Lead us not into temptation but deliver us from evil. For the kingdom, the power, and the glory are yours, now and forever. Amen
> *The Lord's Prayer*

Speaking to God may seem a little strange and uncomfortable to start with, but this will soon pass as you learn to relax in his presence and get to know him better. There is no need to adopt a ritual approach to prayer, although most people fall into the habit of starting and ending most of their prayers in the same way.

For example, they may start by saying 'Dear' followed by 'God' or 'Father' or 'Jesus' or 'Lord', or some combination of these, like 'Dear Lord God'! These ways of addressing God just help us focus our minds on who it is we are actually talking to. Prayers are usually ended with the word 'Amen', which simply means 'So be it' or 'Let it be so'. Before 'Amen' some people may also include the phrase 'in Jesus' name', which reminds us that it is only through Jesus that we are free to talk confidently to God in this direct way.

> the Spirit helps us in our weakness. We do not know what we ought to pray for, but the Spirit himself intercedes for us through wordless groans.
> *Romans 8:26*

The important thing to remember is that God loves you and he is longing for you to spend time with him. He actually knows exactly what is on your mind and in your heart before you say anything, but he wants you to tell

> Rejoice always, pray continually, give thanks in all circumstances; for this is God's will for you in Christ Jesus.
> *1 Thessalonians 5:16–17*

him anyway. The exact words you say don't really matter; God simply wants you to come to him honestly and humbly with trust and faith, and then you will delight his heart.

> Be joyful in hope, patient in affliction, faithful in prayer.
> Romans 12:12

How does God answer prayer?

When we pray God hears us – this is his promise – but what sort of answers are we likely to receive? If the range of our prayers can be extremely diverse and varied, then the answers God gives to our prayers are even more so! Often the answers we get are not the ones we would expect. This is because God is so far above us in his understanding of our needs. He knows best. It is also because God often has a different agenda from our own. Our tendency is to think in the short term and be a little selfish in our requests. In contrast, God's perspective is our eternal good, and not only ours but also that of everyone else around us as well.

> The prayer of a righteous person is powerful and effective.
> James 5:16

This is why it is so important to get to know God better. The more time we spend with him, the more we shall understand what his will is. He reveals his will to us as we read his Word and as we engage with him in prayer. He also makes his will for us clearer through the circumstances and events of our lives. God never gives us anything that is outside his will. The more we understand what his will is, then the more we shall ask for the right things. When we ask according to his will, we shall be given what we ask for. We shall not get what we ask for if we ask for the wrong things, or if we ask with the wrong motives, or we are trying to hide some wrongdoing from God instead of admitting it to him.

Sometimes there will appear to be a long silence in response to our requests. This may be because the timing of our request is wrong, even if we have asked for the right things.

> Then Jesus told his disciples a parable to show them that they should always pray and not give up.
> Luke 18:1

We will need to wait. At other times the apparent silence is because God is testing us to strengthen our faith. When we ask, we are to do so in faith, to believe and not doubt. Jesus taught his disciples to persevere in prayer and so must we. God wants us to seek after him in order to deepen our relationship with him.

God's answers to our prayers can take many forms. When we ask for one thing, he may give us something entirely different. When we ask him to change our circumstances, he may change *us* instead. Here are some of the types of responses we are likely to receive:

- He gives us his peace in the face of difficulty
- He gives us his power and strength
- He gives us courage and confidence
- He keeps us waiting for the right time
- He says 'no'
- He provides our material needs
- He brings healing
- He changes our circumstances
- He tests our sincerity and faith
- He brings clarity to our thinking
- He gives us the conviction to do something

- He gives us the conviction *not* to do something
- He opens a door that had been closed
- He closes a door that appeared to be open
- He causes unexpected events to take place
- He prevents the 'inevitable' from happening
- He gives us skills and abilities
- He gives us spiritual gifts
- He gives us understanding and insight
- He changes our perspective and priorities
- He changes our relationships with other people
- He changes our desires and attitudes
- He changes other people

When we pray, things happen!

**The Christian life is an exciting adventure –
enjoy the journey!**

*Grace and peace to you from God our Father and the Lord Jesus
Christ, who gave himself for our sins to rescue us from the present
evil age, according to the will of our God and Father, to whom
be glory for ever and ever. Amen.*
Galatians 1:3–5

Appendix 1
God's Promises and Words of Encouragement

You are saved

Everyone who calls on the name of the Lord will be saved.

Romans 10:13

he saved us, not because of righteous things we had done, but because of his mercy. He saved us through the washing of rebirth and renewal by the Holy Spirit, whom he poured out on us generously through Jesus Christ our Saviour

Titus 3:5–6

For it is by grace you have been saved, through faith – and this not from yourselves, it is the gift of God – not by works, so that no one can boast.

Ephesians 2:8–9

For he has rescued us from the dominion of darkness and brought us into the kingdom of the Son he loves, in whom we have redemption, the forgiveness of sins.

Colossians 1:13–14

When you were dead in your sins and the uncircumcision of your flesh, God made you alive with Christ. He forgave us all our sins
Colossians 2:13

In him we have redemption through his blood, the forgiveness of sins, in accordance with the riches of God's grace that he lavished on us.
Ephesians 1:7–8

Blessed are those whose transgressions are forgiven, whose sins are covered. Blessed is the one whose sin the Lord will never count against them.
Romans 4:7–8

Therefore, there is now no condemnation for those who are in Christ Jesus, because through Christ Jesus the law of the Spirit who gives life has set you free from the law of sin and death.
Romans 8:1–2

Very truly I tell you, whoever hears my word and believes him who sent me has eternal life and will not be judged but has crossed over from death to life.
John 5:24

Jesus said, 'If you hold to my teaching, you are really my disciples. Then you will know the truth, and the truth will set you free … Very truly I tell you, everyone who sins is a slave to sin … if the Son sets you free, you will be free indeed.'
John 8:31–36

God made him who had no sin to be sin for us, so that in him we might become the righteousness of God.
2 Corinthians 5:21

Christ redeemed us from the curse of the law by becoming a curse for us
Galatians 3:13

Christ Jesus our Lord. In him and through faith in him we may approach God with freedom and confidence.
Ephesians 3:11–12

Let us then approach God's throne of grace with confidence, so that we may receive mercy and find grace to help us in our time of need.
Hebrews 4:16

since we have confidence to enter the Most Holy Place by the blood of Jesus, by a new and living way opened for us … let us draw near to God with a sincere heart and with the full assurance that faith brings
Hebrews 10:19–22

You have eternal life
For God so loved the world that he gave his one and only Son, that whoever believes in him shall not perish but have eternal life.
John 3:16

Very truly I tell you, the one who believes has eternal life.
John 6:47

I give them eternal life, and they shall never perish; no one will snatch them out of my hand.

John 10:28

My Father's house has many rooms; if that were not so, would I have told you that I am going there to prepare a place for you? And if I go and prepare a place for you, I will come back and take you to be with me that you also may be where I am.

John 14:2–3

For we know that if the earthly tent we live in is destroyed, we have a building from God, an eternal house in heaven, not built by human hands.

2 Corinthians 5:1

Now the one who has fashioned us for this very purpose is God, who has given us the Spirit as a deposit, guaranteeing what is to come.

2 Corinthians 5:5

For the Lord himself will come down from heaven, with a loud command, with the voice of the archangel and with the trumpet call of God, and the dead in Christ will rise first. After that, we who are still alive and are left will be caught up together with them in the clouds to meet the Lord in the air. And so we will be with the Lord for ever.

1 Thessalonians 4:16–17

Yet to all who did receive him, to those who believed in his name, he gave the right to become children of God

John 1:12

GOD'S PROMISES AND WORDS OF ENCOURAGEMENT

God sent his Son, born of a woman, born under the law, to redeem those under the law, that we might receive adoption to sonship. Because you are his sons, God sent the Spirit of his Son into our hearts, the Spirit who calls out, 'Abba, Father.' So you are no longer a slave, but God's child; and since you are his child, God has made you also an heir.

Galatians 4:4–7

store up for yourselves treasure in heaven, where moths and vermin do not destroy, and where thieves do not break in and steal. For where your treasure is, there your heart will be also.

Matthew 6:20–21

For the Son of Man is going to come in his Father's glory with his angels, and then he will reward each person according to what they have done.

Matthew 16:27

God's favour and presence rest on you

For I am convinced that neither death nor life, neither angels nor demons, neither the present nor the future, nor any powers, neither height nor depth, nor anything else in all creation, will be able to separate us from the love of God that is in Christ Jesus our Lord.

Romans 8:38–39

I pray that you, being rooted and established in love, may have power, together with all the Lord's holy people, to grasp how wide and long and high and deep is the love of Christ, and to know this love that surpasses knowledge – that you may be filled to the measure of all the fullness of God.

Ephesians 3:17–19

GOD'S LOVE AND TRUTH

Though the mountains be shaken and the hills be removed, yet my unfailing love for you will not be shaken
Isaiah 54:10

I will say of the Lord, 'He is my refuge and my fortress, my God, in whom I trust.'
Psalm 91:2

But blessed is the one who trusts in the Lord, whose confidence is in him.
Jeremiah 17:7

God is our refuge and strength, an ever-present help in trouble.
Psalm 46:1

The Lord himself goes before you and will be with you; he will never leave you nor forsake you. Do not be afraid; do not be discouraged.
Deuteronomy 31:8

God has said, 'Never will I leave you; never will I forsake you.' So we say with confidence, 'The Lord is my helper; I will not be afraid.'
Hebrews 13:5–6

And surely I am with you always, to the very end of the age.
Matthew 28:20

The eternal God is your refuge, and underneath are the everlasting arms.
Deuteronomy 33:27

GOD'S PROMISES AND WORDS OF ENCOURAGEMENT

Praise be to the God and Father of our Lord Jesus Christ, the Father of compassion and the God of all comfort, who comforts us in all our troubles
2 Corinthians 1:3–4

Cast all your anxiety on him because he cares for you.
1 Peter 5:7

Peace I leave with you; my peace I give you. I do not give to you as the world gives. Do not let your hearts be troubled and do not be afraid.
John 14:27

Do not be anxious about anything, but in every situation, by prayer and petition, with thanksgiving, present your requests to God. And the peace of God, which transcends all understanding, will guard your hearts and your minds in Christ Jesus.
Philippians 4:6–7

God watches over you

The LORD is my rock, my fortress and my deliverer; my God is my rock, in whom I take refuge, my shield and the horn of my salvation, my stronghold.
Psalm 18:2

Blessed are those whose help is the God of Jacob, whose hope is in the LORD their God. He is the Maker of heaven and earth, the sea, and everything in them – he remains faithful for ever.
Psalm 146:5–6

GOD'S LOVE AND TRUTH

So do not fear, for I am with you; do not be dismayed, for I am your God. I will strengthen you and help you; I will uphold you with my righteous right hand.

Isaiah 41:10

Do you not know? Have you not heard? The Lord is the everlasting God, the Creator of the ends of the earth. He will not grow tired or weary, and his understanding no one can fathom. He gives strength to the weary and increases the power of the weak. Even youths grow tired and weary, and young men stumble and fall; but those who hope in the Lord will renew their strength. They will soar on wings like eagles; they will run and not grow weary, they will walk and not be faint.

Isaiah 40:28–31

the Lord is faithful, and he will strengthen you and protect you from the evil one.

2 Thessalonians 3:3

you, who through faith are shielded by God's power until the coming of the salvation that is ready to be revealed in the last time.

1 Peter 1:4–5

your Father knows what you need before you ask him.

Matthew 6:8

And my God will meet all your needs according to the riches of his glory in Christ Jesus.

Philippians 4:19

the same Lord is Lord of all and richly blesses all who call on him
Romans 10:12

'For I know the plans I have for you,' declares the LORD, 'plans to prosper you and not to harm you, plans to give you hope and a future.'
Jeremiah 29:11

In their hearts humans plan their course, but the LORD establishes their steps.
Proverbs 16:9

I am the LORD your God, who teaches you what is best for you, who directs you in the way you should go.
Isaiah 48:17

God will empower you

Do you not know that your bodies are temples of the Holy Spirit, who is in you, whom you have received from God?
1 Corinthians 6:19

This is how we know that we live in him and he in us: he has given us of his Spirit.
1 John 4:13

God's love has been poured out into our hearts through the Holy Spirit, who has been given to us.
Romans 5:5

For the Spirit God gave us does not make us timid, but gives us power, love and self-discipline.
2 Timothy 1:7

I pray that out of his glorious riches he may strengthen you with power through his Spirit in your inner being
Ephesians 3:16

I keep asking that the God of our Lord Jesus Christ, the glorious Father, may give you the Spirit of wisdom and revelation, so that you may know him better.
Ephesians 1:17

the Advocate, the Holy Spirit, whom the Father will send in my name, will teach you all things
John 14:26

But when he, the Spirit of truth, comes, he will guide you into all the truth.
John 16:13

the Spirit helps us in our weakness. We do not know what we ought to pray for, but the Spirit himself intercedes for us through wordless groans.
Romans 8:26

true worshippers will worship the Father in the Spirit and in truth, for they are the kind of worshippers the Father seeks. God is spirit, and his worshippers must worship in the Spirit and in truth.
John 4:23–24

So I say, live by the Spirit, and you will not gratify the desires of the flesh. For the flesh desires what is contrary to the Spirit, and the Spirit what is contrary to the flesh. They are in conflict with each other
Galatians 5:16–17

Resist the devil, and he will flee from you.
James 4:7

No temptation has overtaken you except what is common to mankind. And God is faithful; he will not let you be tempted beyond what you can bear. But when you are tempted, he will also provide a way out so that you can endure it.
1 Corinthians 10:13

The Lord will rescue me from every evil attack and will bring me safely to his heavenly kingdom.
2 Timothy 4:18

His divine power has given us everything we need for a godly life
2 Peter 1:3

And we all, who with unveiled faces contemplate the Lord's glory, are being transformed into his image with ever-increasing glory, which comes from the Lord, who is the Spirit.
2 Corinthians 3:18

There are different kinds of gifts, but the same Spirit … All these are the work of one and the same Spirit, and he distributes them to each one, just as he determines.
1 Corinthians 12:4, 11

But each of you has your own gift from God; one has this gift, another has that.

1 Corinthians 7:7

Now, Lord, consider their threats and enable your servants to speak your word with great boldness. Stretch out your hand to heal and perform signs and wonders through the name of your holy servant Jesus.

Acts 4:29–30

you will receive power when the Holy Spirit comes on you; and you will be my witnesses in Jerusalem, and in all Judea and Samaria, and to the ends of the earth.

Acts 1:8

To him who is able to keep you from stumbling and to present you before his glorious presence without fault and with great joy – to the only God our Saviour be glory, majesty, power and authority, through Jesus Christ our Lord, before all ages, now and for evermore! Amen.

Jude 24–25

Appendix 2

God's Instructions For Christian Living

Note: 'TC' below denotes the Ten Commandments

Love God
Love the Lord your God with all your heart and with all your soul and with all your strength and with all your mind
Luke 10:27

what does the Lord your God ask of you but to fear the Lord your God, to walk in obedience to him, to love him, to serve the Lord your God with all your heart and with all your soul, and to observe the Lord's commands
Deuteronomy 10:12–13

You shall have no other gods before me.
You shall not make for yourself an image in the form of anything in heaven above or on the earth beneath or in the waters below. You shall not bow down to them or worship them
Exodus 20:3–5 (TC 1–2)

You shall not misuse the name of the Lord your God
Exodus 20:7 (TC 3)

Remember the Sabbath day by keeping it holy.
Exodus 20:8 (TC 4)

You have made known to me the path of life; you will fill me with joy in your presence, with eternal pleasures at your right hand.
Psalm 16:11

Let the message of Christ dwell among you richly as you teach and admonish one another with all wisdom through psalms, hymns, and songs from the Spirit, singing to God with gratitude in your hearts.
Colossians 3:16

if you call out for insight and cry aloud for understanding, and if you look for it as for silver and search for it as for hidden treasure, then you will understand the fear of the Lord and find the knowledge of God. For the Lord gives wisdom; from his mouth come knowledge and understanding.
Proverbs 2:3–6

Through Jesus, therefore, let us continually offer to God a sacrifice of praise – the fruit of lips that openly profess his name.
Hebrews 13:15

Worship the Lord with gladness; come before him with joyful songs.
Psalm 100:2

Devote yourselves to prayer, being watchful and thankful.
Colossians 4:2

Love others
Love your neighbour as yourself.
Luke 10:27

Do to others as you would have them do to you.
Luke 6:31

Do nothing out of selfish ambition or vain conceit. Rather, in humility value others above yourselves, not looking to your own interests but each of you to the interests of the others.
Philippians 2:3–4

No one should seek their own good, but the good of others.
1 Corinthians 10:24

Therefore, as we have opportunity, let us do good to all people, especially to those who belong to the family of believers.
Galatians 6:10

We who are strong ought to bear with the failings of the weak and not to please ourselves. Each of us should please our neighbours for their good, to build them up.
Romans 15:1–2

Honour your father and your mother
Exodus 20:12 (TC 5)

Live as children of light (for the fruit of the light consists in all goodness, righteousness and truth) and find out what pleases the Lord.

Ephesians 5:8–10

Therefore, as God's chosen people, holy and dearly loved, clothe yourselves with compassion, kindness, humility, gentleness and patience.

Colossians 3:12

have sincere love for each other, love one another deeply, from the heart.

1 Peter 1:22

Be devoted to one another in love. Honour one another above yourselves.

Romans 12:10

all of you, be like-minded, be sympathetic, love one another, be compassionate and humble.

1 Peter 3:8

Grow in knowledge, faith and obedience

And without faith it is impossible to please God, because anyone who comes to him must believe that he exists and that he rewards those who earnestly seek him.

Hebrews 11:6

GOD'S INSTRUCTIONS FOR CHRISTIAN LIVING

Trust in the LORD with all your heart and lean not on your own understanding; in all your ways submit to him and he will make your paths straight.
Proverbs 3:5–6

the one who believes in him will never be put to shame.
Romans 9:33

For you were once darkness, but now you are light in the Lord. Live as children of light ... and find out what pleases the Lord.
Ephesians 5:8–10

we have not stopped praying for you. We continually ask God to fill you with the knowledge of his will through all the wisdom and understanding that the Spirit gives, so that you may live a life worthy of the Lord and please him in every way
Colossians 1:9–10

Your word is a lamp for my feet, a light on my path.
Psalm 119:105

Do not merely listen to the word, and so deceive yourselves. Do what it says.
James 1:22

Jesus replied, 'Anyone who loves me will obey my teaching.'
John 14:23

Therefore let us move beyond the elementary teachings about Christ and be taken forward to maturity
Hebrews 6:1

Do not conform to the pattern of this world, but be transformed by the renewing of your mind.
Romans 12:2

I seek you with all my heart; do not let me stray from your commands. I have hidden your word in my heart that I might not sin against you.
Psalm 119:10–11

Serve God
Therefore, I urge you, brothers and sisters, in view of God's mercy, to offer your bodies as a living sacrifice, holy and pleasing to God – this is your true and proper worship.
Romans 12:1

For we are God's handiwork, created in Christ Jesus to do good works, which God prepared in advance for us to do.
Ephesians 2:10

Each of you should use whatever gift you have received to serve others, as faithful stewards of God's grace in its various forms.
1 Peter 4:10

Never be lacking in zeal, but keep your spiritual fervour, serving the Lord.
Romans 12:11

How, then, can they call on the one they have not believed in? And how can they believe in the one of whom they have not heard? And how can they hear without someone preaching to them? And how can anyone preach unless they are sent?
Romans 10:14–15

He said to them, 'Go into all the world and preach the gospel to all creation.'
Mark 16:15

Always be prepared to give an answer to everyone who asks you to give the reason for the hope that you have. But do this with gentleness and respect
1 Peter 3:15

And pray in the Spirit on all occasions with all kinds of prayers and requests. With this in mind, be alert and always keep on praying for all the Lord's people.
Ephesians 6:18

I urge, then, first of all, that petitions, prayers, intercession and thanksgiving be made for all people
1 Timothy 2:1

Freely you have received; freely give.
Matthew 10:8

Each of you should give what you have decided in your heart to give, not reluctantly or under compulsion, for God loves a cheerful giver.
2 Corinthians 9:7

Overcome sin

As obedient children, do not conform to the evil desires you had when you lived in ignorance. But just as he who called you is holy, so be holy in all you do.

1 Peter 1:14–15

For the grace of God has appeared that offers salvation to all people. It teaches us to say 'No' to ungodliness and worldly passions, and to live self-controlled, upright and godly lives

Titus 2:11–12

Submit yourselves, then, to God. Resist the devil, and he will flee from you. Come near to God and he will come near to you.

James 4:7–8

Watch and pray so that you will not fall into temptation. The spirit is willing, but the flesh is weak.

Mark 14:38

You were taught, with regard to your former way of life, to put off your old self, which is being corrupted by its deceitful desires; to be made new in the attitude of your minds; and to put on the new self, created to be like God in true righteousness and holiness.

Ephesians 4:22–24

Put to death, therefore, whatever belongs to your earthly nature: sexual immorality, impurity, lust, evil desires and greed, which is idolatry. Because of these, the wrath of God is coming. You used to walk in these ways, in the life you once lived. But now you must also rid yourselves of all such things as these: anger, rage, malice, slander, and filthy language from your lips. Do not lie to each other,

since you have taken off your old self with its practices and have put on the new self, which is being renewed in knowledge in the image of its Creator.
Colossians 3:5–10

The acts of the flesh are obvious: sexual immorality, impurity and debauchery; idolatry and witchcraft; hatred, discord, jealousy, fits of rage, selfish ambition, dissensions, factions and envy; drunkenness, orgies, and the like. I warn you, as I did before, that those who live like this will not inherit the kingdom of God. But the fruit of the Spirit is love, joy, peace, forbearance, kindness, goodness, faithfulness, gentleness and self-control. Against such things there is no law.
Galatians 5:19–23

You shall not murder.
You shall not commit adultery.
You shall not steal.
You shall not give false testimony …
You shall not covet
Exodus 20:13–17 (TC 6–10)

If we confess our sins, he is faithful and just and will forgive us our sins and purify us from all unrighteousness.
1 John 1:9

Therefore confess your sins to each other
James 5:16

if you hold anything against anyone, forgive them, so that your Father in heaven may forgive you your sins.

Mark 11:25

Be kind and compassionate to one another, forgiving each other, just as in Christ God forgave you.

Ephesians 4:32

the Most High ... is kind to the ungrateful and wicked. Be merciful, just as your Father is merciful.

Luke 6:35–36